How to Become a
Sweet
Old Lady
Instead of a
Grumpy Old Grouch

How to Become a Sweet Old Lady Instead of a Grumpy Old Grouch

Marilynn Carlson Webber

ZondervanPublishingHouse

Grand Rapids, Michigan

A Division of HarperCollinsPublishers

How to Become a Sweet Old Lady Instead of a Grumpy Old Grouch
Copyright © 1996 by Marilynn Carlson Webber

Requests for information should be addressed to:

 ZondervanPublishingHouse
Grand Rapids, Michigan 49530

Library of Congress Cataloging-in-Publication Data

Webber, Marilynn Carlson.
    How to become a sweet old lady instead of a grumpy old grouch /
Marilynn Carlson Webber.
        p.   cm.
    ISBN: 0-310-20716-9
    1. Women—Conduct of life.   I. Title.
BJ1610.W44   1996
248.8'43—dc20   96-9079
                                                                          CIP

Interior design by Sherri L. Hoffman

Printed in the United States of America

96 97 98 99 00 01 02 03 / ❖ DH/ 10 9 8 7 6 5 4 3 2 1

*To all the sweet old ladies who through the years
have shared their secrets with me*

*To my grandmother, Emma Carlson,
and my mother, Alice Carlson,
who first guided me on the path
to Christian maturity*

*To Gertrude Bardarson, Lucille Calvert,
Helen McLean, and Margaret Sharp,
who have been role models*

Contents

Preface

This book is for women of all ages in response to requests from women of all ages. It's not a book about aging. You won't find advice about where to live in retirement, what to do about Medicare, or counsel about long-term nursing insurance.

It is a book about how to find happiness and purpose in your life, whatever your age may be. It is a book about learning to cope with the everyday issues of life. It is a book that challenges you to make those decisions that will make you a mature person. After all, what is the basic characteristic of a "sweet old lady"? When you put all her traits together, it is another way of saying she is a mature, wise woman.

In my research I have discovered the road to maturity begins with our earliest choices. Whether we recognize it or not, we are on our way to becoming a sweet old lady or a grumpy old grouch right now. The good news is that change is always possible. The bad news is that old habits are hard to change. The longer we wait to begin healthy new patterns, the harder it is. No one ever plans to end up as a mean old lady. Almost without exception the happy older woman is the one who has been practicing the art of living for years.

Such maturity is made up of many individual traits that are a result of our daily choices. This book describes several that are important. Although I have read extensively on the subject for years (and I hope some of that will come through), I have found the greatest help in my personal pilgrimage was to observe women who faced the same problems I was facing and who were positive examples. Today we call these women role models, a term that was not widely used when I began my study.

I enjoy reading about famous women. Their stories inspire me, but a little voice inside me always suggests I could never be a Mother Teresa! The examples that help me the most are those of my neighbors, friends, ordinary people. These are the accounts I share with you in this book. I trust as you read these snatches of real life your response will be like mine. "What a great example! I want to be like that, too. If they could do it, I can, too, with the help of God."

This is a call to grow up, to stop being in pigtails, to take responsibility for your life. The goal is to become that sweet old lady. The process is to begin now, becoming a mature woman, whatever your age may be. The reward is one you do not have to wait for until you are old. The process of becoming carries its own reward—bringing true happiness as we grow.

For years I have been speaking on this topic to women's groups. It is a fun topic about a serious subject, and it has been my most requested talk for mother-daughter banquets where young girls as well as their mothers have attended. I have been asked to speak on this subject to women's clubs, church groups, college classes, retirement homes, auxiliaries of all kinds, and hospital caregivers. Many have asked for the substance of these talks to be printed for further study or to share with others. I thank these women for their encouragement.

I express my special thanks to Ruth Smith, Margaret Sharp, Virginia Cosner Shiffer, and Cynthia Curts, who have been prayer partners in the writing of this book. They have been examples to me of caring, wise, mature women. In time they will become sweet old ladies.

My sincere thanks goes to the staff of Zondervan Publishing House for their help and guidance. Especially helpful has been Lyn Cryderman's belief in this project from its inception. Our editor, Lori Walburg, has been of real assistance in working through our manuscript and preparing it for publication.

My husband, William, is my best friend and most enthusiastic writing coach. In many ways, small and great, he polished this manuscript and brought it to perfection. I am deeply grateful for his part in my life and my work.

My special thanks to those women whose stories are told in this book and who have been such an inspiration to me and to others in their quiet ways. Most of all, thanks to our Lord Jesus Christ who calls us from what we are to what we should become.

ONE

Secrets Too Good to Keep

A sweet old lady is constantly changing for the better. A grumpy old grouch tries to change other people.

I'm sure no one would ever guess, but I am a grandmother! I have three darling grandchildren, and I've learned to love the questions grandchildren can ask. A friend told me her grandson asked, "Grandmother, how old are you?"

My friend answered, "Grandson, there are some things you don't ask a woman, and her age is one of them."

Later the boy asked, "Grandmother, how much do you weigh?" Again the grandmother explained there are some things you do not ask a woman—especially her weight!

Some time passed, and the boy returned and inquired, "Grandmother, there are two beds in your bedroom. Why don't you and Grandfather sleep together?"

The grandmother replied, "There are some things you don't ask a grandmother, and that's one of them. Go see what you can find to play with."

A little while later the boy returned with a smile on his face. "Grandmother," he said proudly, "I've been playing with your purse. I found your driver's license, and now I know the answers to all my questions. On your driver's license under "age," it says you are sixty-two years old. Under "weight" it says

13

you are one hundred sixty-five pounds. And under "sex," it says you got an F!"

Some things a lady doesn't tell, but in this book I am going to share some secrets I have learned that are too good to keep. As a young minister's wife, I found some wonderful people in our church. I was also appalled to discover some difficult people as well. Although there are nice people and problem people of all ages, I observed that the differences tend to be more pronounced as people grow older. Some older women everyone loves to be with. Others, people try to avoid.

I became fascinated with the question: Why does one woman become a sweet old lady while another becomes a grumpy old grouch? Through the years I observed the women around me. As a pastor's wife I listened as many poured out their hearts to me. I learned from the wise counsel of women I came to admire. Perhaps I profited the most from the hard lessons I learned as my life was touched by those who were unhappy, bitter, and mean-spirited. I read widely on the subject. When I received invitations to speak, I began to share what I had learned. I gained new insights from the many people who talked with me after I had spoken to their group on "How to Become a Sweet Old Lady Instead of a Grumpy Old Grouch."

My files grew as I collected wonderful, practical advice distilled in words and phrases that anyone could understand. I became convinced that most people don't need a psychiatrist, but we all need to have a clear idea of the person we want to become. Then we need an understanding of how to become that person. As William Bennett points out in *The Book of Virtues*, virtues are seldom learned by precept. They are most easily grasped by examples of people in real-life situations. As I realized how many inspiring stories I had collected, I knew I had to write this book and share those things that had so profoundly affected my life.

I do not claim to be a sweet old lady. Parts of me find it easier to be a grumpy old grouch. But my goal is to make progress each day toward being the person God would have me be. I know he wants me to become a sweet old lady rather than a grumpy old grouch. The path I am taking I walk with his help, using the guidance and example of many who have made more progress than I.

Usually when I talk, people immediately think of people they know, both the sweet old ladies and the grumpy old grouches. It's easy to see this in others. But which are you becoming? Are you growing sweeter as the years go by? Or are you well on the way to becoming a grumpy old grouch?

This question is important. The choices we make now affect the way we will be later. The United States Congress made a $500,000 grant for social scientists to study why some older people are happy and pleasant to be around while others are miserable and difficult to be with. The study made it clear: A person's characteristics tend to become more accentuated as life goes on. The sweet people become sweeter; the selfish people become more self-centered. I'm not sure it was necessary to spend a half million dollars of tax money to discover this truism, but it is nice to know that what we all suspected has been confirmed by a scientific study.

The study missed one important fact, however. People can and do change. Some pleasant, happy people well on their way to becoming sweet old ladies have had their lives touched by disappointments or tragedies. The earlier spirit of loveliness gave way to a growing bitterness. And the opposite is also true. People can and do change for the better. This book will give case studies of miserable women and how they were transformed into women of joy and beauty.

For ten happy years my husband, Bill, and I served a church in Springfield, Missouri, the gateway to the Ozarks. People in Springfield like to tell the story about the day a mountain man came to the city for the first time. His curiosity had gotten the best of him, and he came to see if buildings several stories tall really existed.

He walked into the town square and saw it was true. He stood in front of Heers Department Store and marveled at the displays in the windows. When he came to the entrance of the store, the door opened before him like magic. What a surprise! No one had told him about automatic doors. He stopped at the cosmetic counter, where a woman was getting a cosmetic makeover.

Then he noticed a strange thing on the wall. There were doors that opened and closed. Zeke had never seen an elevator and had no idea what it was. He watched with fascination as a wrinkled old lady hobbled into that box. Zeke watched as the doors closed. A minute later the doors opened, and out stepped a beautiful young lady. The mountain man rushed out of the store, exclaiming, "I've got to get my wife, Millie, and put her in that box!" It never occurred to Zeke that he could make wonderful changes in *his* life. His only thought was that his wife needed changing!

I wrote an article for *Guideposts* magazine about a friend who taught me much about growing old gracefully. In the back of the magazine is a feature that gives a sketch of the writers in each issue. In it they said that I talked on "How to Become a Sweet Old Lady Instead of a Grumpy Old Grouch." One woman wrote, "Please send me a copy of your talk, quick! I need to give it to my mother-in-law." That's the wrong idea.

Another person wrote, "I'm a forty-two-year-old grouch, but I do want to become a sweet old lady. Send your message quick!" That's the right idea. The good news is that even if you are well on your way to becoming a grumpy old grouch, you can change to become a sweet old lady. That's the journey I am taking. Won't you join me?

TWO

❧ ❧

Create Your Own Party

A sweet old lady takes the initiative. A grumpy old grouch complains that nothing interesting is happening.

I first met Bardy at a church picnic when I was feeling lost. Bill and I had just moved to Seattle after ten wonderful years in Springfield, Missouri. Although this was not our first move, and although I felt that God had called my husband to be the senior pastor of the Seattle First Baptist Church, the move was very difficult. For the first time, I felt I lacked the energy to start over.

I had been dealt so many losses in such a short time. My mother had died. Our two children had left the nest and were thousands of miles away at college. Going to Seattle meant moving half a continent away from my close friends. I loved the church in Springfield, and during our ten-year ministry there, I had developed close ties with several people and felt that I really belonged.

There were a few hundred people at the church picnic at Carcreek Park. I was glad for the excellent turnout, but I couldn't help thinking that back in Springfield I would have known everyone. Here I could put only a few names and faces together.

I was relieved when an older woman purposely made her way over to sit and talk with me. She was tall and vivacious, with silver hair and a touch of a Swedish accent. "My name is

Gertrude Bardarson," she said, "but my friends call me Bardy."
She was genuinely interested in what I had to say, and she
often laughed as she spoke. Before she left she said, "We'll
have to get together for dinner sometime."

"I'd love that," I said sincerely. I remember thinking she
would never get around to inviting us.

The next day the phone rang. It was Bardy, setting a date for
dinner the following week. And what a dinner it was! She had
gone to the Pike Street Market for fresh salmon. Then she had
cooked it with care and garnished it so it looked like a page from
a gourmet magazine. The entire meal was a change from the
company meals we had become accustomed to in the Midwest,
and it was a delightful introduction to the Pacific Northwest.

As I helped her clear the table, I was surprised to hear
myself confiding my losses to her. I caught myself as we
reached the kitchen. "I'm sorry," I said. "You have lived here
for many years and have so many friends. I don't know if you
can understand."

Her eyes were sympathetic. "Oh, Marilynn, I do understand. Even better, I know a secret taught to me by my immi-
grant mother. You see, she came over from Sweden, away
from her family and friends to an arranged marriage. It's fair to
say the marriage was not what my mother had hoped. My parents weren't suited for each other. Yet she lived a full and
happy life—happy of her own choosing."

"At a low point in my own life, my mother told me her
secret," Bardy continued. "My sadness was the opposite of hers.
I married a wonderful man. I felt like a schoolgirl each time I
saw him coming home from work. He became the superinten-
dent of schools in Carmel, California. Several years after we had
moved there, he kissed me good-bye and went to work. I never
dreamed that before the day was over I'd become a widow. He
died of a heart attack. He was only thirty-three."

After her husband's death, Bardy had become very ill, even
wondering if she wanted to go on living. Being a widow with
two small sons was not what she had hoped for.

"It might sound funny at first, but this is what my mother told me: Create your own party. Instead of moaning about the bad hand life has dealt you, be thankful for what you do have and share it with those around you. You see, creating happiness for others in turn blesses you. You needn't wait for a special day. For example, today I could have been home alone, but it is so much more fun to reach out and make new friends. There's always fulfilling work to be done and new friends to make."

Create your own party! What wonderful advice. How it can change your life. It's so simple, and best of all, anyone can do it.

Our British Tea Party

Our family has wonderful memories of the summer we spent in Brighton, England. Bill exchanged pulpits with Jack Hair, a British pastor. He lived in our home and pastored our church in the United States. We lived in their manse. Bill preached and prayed, led the church, visited the sick, and had many funerals.

What we treasure most are the memories of the times we spent in English homes. We loved the roast beef dinner with Yorkshire pudding in the elegant house of the Habens. Even more, we enjoyed going to Mrs. Hardingham's simple flat.

Mrs. Hardingham was a pensioner with a very limited income. Her flat was so small that our family of four could hardly fit into it. But what a wonderful time we had when she created a party! Although she planned a special time for us, she spent very little on the meal.

We didn't know what to expect when she asked us to bring our two children at four, then return for the dinner at six. We discovered the reason when we came to dinner. Mrs. Hardingham had worked in a bakery. She spent the two hours teaching our children how to change a simple, inexpensive meal into a party our family has never forgotten. I recall that the meal ended with cupcakes for dessert. She had coached our son and daughter, and they had transformed the cupcakes into beautiful butterflies.

While others in similar circumstances stayed at home alone, feeling too old or too poor, Mrs. Hardingham opened her heart and her home, and we were all blessed.

Make Life Interesting

Do you catch the idea? Creating your own party means taking the initiative to make your life interesting. Don't wait for others! Abraham Lincoln was right when he said, "A person is about as happy as he decides to be." Decide to have fun and make your life interesting.

The grumpy old grouch complains there is nothing to do. She doesn't get invited to parties. The woman on her way to becoming a sweet old lady creates her own party and invites others to come. She doesn't stop just because her guests may not invite her back. She enjoys the planning and the fun of the party, knowing that it does good things for those who attend, even if they do not return the invitation. After all, why should we let them keep us from having our own party? Especially, let's not allow ourselves to become bitter, brooding over their lack of response. Part of the fun can be enticing a Scrooge to enjoy Christmas.

Once in a Blue Moon

You can create a party for every occasion or none at all. People often are intrigued most by the affair that is unexpected. Our daughter invited friends to a blue moon party. Everyone has heard the expression, "once in a blue moon." Few people know that a blue moon is when the full moon appears for the second time in a month. Because it takes twenty-eight days for the moon to go through its cycle, this doesn't happen often. Guests were invited to come in something they would wear only once in a blue moon. What fun! The food included things one would serve only occasionally, and the activities that evening were things people enjoyed but seldom did. It is hard to resist an invitation to such an event, and it was a topic of conversation for days before and after the event.

Dorothy Goodwin, who lived in a retirement community, invited her friends to a tea in honor of Emily Dickinson's birthday. It cost Dorothy less than five dollars for the tea, cookies, and napkins. She read a few of Emily Dickinson's short poems, and the rest of the time was spent in conversation over teacups. It was the talk of Mount Rubidoux Manor.

Of course, you don't have to throw a party in the dictionary sense of the word. You can simply invite people to go with your doing whatever you enjoy. It's more fun taking a drive to look at the daffodils when you share the experience with another. In every community there is somewhere to go that people plan to see sometime, but most people never do. It may be a local landmark, a public garden, or even a new store or shopping center. Are people in your town talking about those fancy new coffees? You may think it crazy to pay $2.50 for a cup of espresso, but why not try it once and see what it's like? People will love you for saying, "Let's go!" And if the first ones you invite cannot or will not go, keep asking. Create your own party.

It can be a party for one—for me, myself, and I. After all, "one" is a whole number! My friend, Sally Bleck, lives alone. She does have a grown son and enjoys the time they spend together, but most evenings she is alone at dinner. With some regularity, Sally plans a party for herself. Why not? She spends more time than usual cooking a favorite meal. She sets the table with a cloth and her best dishes and silver. She brings in flowers from her yard. She makes an evening of the experience, both pampering herself and feeling pampered. She counts her blessings. Best of all, Sally says, she is aware of God's presence with her. God is always with us, true, even when we catch the evening news while we eat a TV dinner. But we become aware of his presence in a different way when we create our own party for one.

Do you catch the idea? Whoever you are, wherever you may be, your life can be satisfying and enjoyable. To be bored and lonely is a choice. It is not your best choice, and it certainly is not your only choice. Life can be fun and rewarding, but often it will only be that way if you take the initiative. Don't while away your days waiting for others to change your circumstances. Create your own party!

THREE

Accentuate the Positive

A sweet old lady admires the roses. A grumpy old grouch complains about the thorns.

*H*onestly, I was not prepared. My husband, Bill, was the new senior pastor of the Seattle First Baptist Church. Early in the morning he had led the Easter sunrise service our church hosted high above the city in the space needle. After an inspiring service, I had joined the worshipers as we filled the revolving Space Needle Restaurant for breakfast. The excitement of the resurrection service and the warmth and friendliness of the people had made this an unforgettable experience.

Next came the Easter services in the beautiful church sanctuary. The sun streaming through the stained glass windows, the magnificent sounds of the great organ, and the triumphant voices of the choir all blended to create the setting for the greatest message of all: The Lord is risen!

Although he had appeared relaxed through the many activities of Easter morning, I knew Bill had to be physically and emotionally exhausted after the busy morning. But his concern was for those who had not been able to attend the Easter services. He asked me to join him and take lilies from the church to some of the shut-ins who lived at Hilltop House, our church's retirement home.

Betty's apartment was on the tenth floor. "Come in," she said. Those were the only pleasant words we would hear.

Immediately she began to complain, especially about her family. People didn't come to visit her, she groused, and when they did, they didn't stay long.

Just then there was a knock at the door. Her son and his family came bearing gifts. Betty didn't take the time to acknowledge their gifts. Instead she began a tirade in front of her pastor, complaining that her son didn't treat his mother right. "Last Sunday was Palm Sunday, and you didn't come to see me," she shouted. Instead of enjoying their Easter visit, she grumbled the entire time. When we left, Bill said, "I can see why her son doesn't come to visit more often." A negative attitude drives people away.

Being Positive Attracts Others

When Dewey, my husband's father, died, we took him back to Springfield, Missouri, to be buried next to his wife. After the graveside service, Bill and I stopped by to visit Helen McLain, a friend we had known when we had lived in Springfield. The past year had been difficult for Helen. Her grown son had died. The husband she had loved so deeply, died. We thought it would be a difficult call to make. But Helen greeted us warmly. Instead of complaining bitterly about her losses, she said with wonder in her voice, "I can't believe that in the time of your grief you would take time to visit me." As she talked about the husband and son she had recently lost to death, she recounted the many things she had to be thankful about them. She shared her memories with an attitude of gratitude for what she had. Bill and I left, feeling blessed by our visit and eager to keep in touch.

My husband was faithful in his pastoral work and visited with Betty in the retirement home on many occasions. "Is Betty still complaining?" I asked him one day.

"Yes," he replied. "I try to bring a bright spot in her day and talk about things that are interesting and encouraging, but she always brings the subject back to her two pet peeves—the food in the retirement home, and the fact that people don't come to visit her often enough."

"You know why they don't come more often," I said. "Have you ever talked with her about her attitude? Someone needs to."

"I waited until I had gotten to know her and for Betty to come to feel comfortable with me," Bill replied. "One day she asked why I thought people didn't come. As compassionately as I could, I talked with her about her negative attitude. I explained how her constant complaints turned people off."

"Has she changed?" I asked hopefully.

My husband shook his head sadly. "Not at all. You see, Betty doesn't see herself as a negative person. She believes it's terrible the way she is treated and that she has every right to complain."

Almost no one admits to being negative. We become experts at rationalization. We tell ourselves that we are just being realistic—things are bad for us. We excuse our constant complaining by denying that we are a complainer. We're just being honest, we're sharing, we're being open to others. After all, isn't that what a person should do?

Of course, we need to be genuine, to share hurts and problems with our close friends and family. We are to bear one another's burdens in a Christian spirit that is helpful and beneficial to all. But the majority of us are often guilty of ruminating on our hardships and telling our woes at every opportunity, or, if not at every opportunity, at least more often than others would like and more often than is beneficial for us. The person on her way to becoming a sweet old lady is the one who is usually fun to be with, who smiles often, who affirms the people she is with, and who accentuates the positive. We are moving toward being that grumpy old grouch when we choose to be contrary, cross, cranky, disagreeable, and ornery. Because becoming critical is easy to do, we would be wise to touch base regularly with a trusted friend or family member and ask, "Am I fun to live with?"

Bitter or Better?

It was an unforgettable moment. The angel flag was flying outside my house as I welcomed a group arriving for tea. "Welcome to the house of angels," I said as I introduced myself and the guests filed into my home filled with my collection of more than thirty-five hundred angel figures.

"Hello, I'm Barbara Kincaid," a cheerful voice replied.

I caught my breath, speechless for a moment. The woman greeting me had her hair swept up in a Gibson girl hairdo. Her dress was appropriate for afternoon tea in 1995, but she would have looked equally in place at a Victorian tea party. Not only was the dress a Victorian style, but Barbara's high cheekbones, smiling, demure eyes, and hourglass figure also bore a strong resemblance to the pictures I had seen of Victorian women. During the tea at my home we became better acquainted. When Barbara extended an invitation to tea at her house, Bill and I were eager to go.

A few days later, Barbara welcomed us to her home. It was a new house, built in the Victorian style, complete with a butler's pantry. Crossing the threshold, we felt as though we had returned to a time one hundred years ago. We enjoyed the serenity of afternoon tea, including warm savories, scones with Devon cream, and pastries fresh from Barbara's oven.

My attention was drawn to an unusual piece hanging on the wall. "What is it?" I asked. "Does it have a story?"

"Indeed it does," Barbara replied. "It's a mourning frame. This one is dated 1905. This is the way families honored the dead in the nineteenth and early twentieth centuries."

The elaborately carved mourning frame held a memorial card with hand-painted flowers, the dove of peace, and the anchor, a symbol of the Navy.

"The young man in the picture is my son, Bill," Barbara explained. "He was a casualty in Operation Desert Storm when he was twenty-eight years old. It was especially hard for me because he was my only son and we had been so close."

Barbara paused. "So many people tried to help at the time of my loss. But then, after Bill's funeral, their lives went back to normal while mine remained shattered. I closed my vintage clothing store and put my antiques and clothing collection in storage. The days seemed unbearably long. Even my husband couldn't comfort me. Nothing seemed to matter anymore.

"It was then I realized I had a conscious choice to make. I could not change that my son had died. But I could choose how I would react to it. I could either grow bitter or better. I could continue to be devastated by my grief, or I could get on with my life and grow more compassionate. I could be thankful for what I had, rather than dwell on what I had lost.

"I knew which decision God wanted me to make. It was the same choice my son would want me to make. I claimed God's promises to comfort and help me and stepped out in faith to rebuild my life. It was then I discovered God's grace in a new and vital way."

After making her choice, Barbara and Dave bought property near the Cajon Pass in Southern California. Together they designed and built their new Victorian home, complete with authentic antiques circa 1880 to 1900. Over the carriage house Barbara has a studio for her vintage clothing and fashion memorabilia from Scarlett O'Hara to Jackie Kennedy.

Today Barbara prepares and serves English Victorian afternoon teas in her home. Her guests enjoy the warm atmosphere of a gracious bygone era when the ritual and ceremony of afternoon tea was an art. If someone asks about the mourning frame, Barbara tells them about her son's death, her grief, and her decision. "When disappointments and hurts invade our lives," Barbara points out, "we must choose either to become bitter or better. It was when I chose to work through my bitterness that I discovered God's grace." Today Barbara has found the comfort of God and is able to comfort others.

Such decisions are not optional. We must each choose how we will respond to life's hurts. The decisions we make result not only in the way we approach life but also how others respond to us.

A Tale of Two Women

Fran and I were members of a small prayer group. Fran always looked her best, and her best was something most women would die for. After people met her, they commented on her good looks. Fran was a willing worker. She could be counted on to help in her church, clubs, and neighborhood. Fran was also a widow. Her husband had died early but had left her with provisions so she could live comfortably. She had so much going for her.

But Fran seldom smiles. Her friends all know why. One thing is missing, and Fran will not be happy without it. She wants to be married. It is not that she misses her late husband so much. Rather she feels incomplete. She was brought up in a culture that expected a woman to be married, and she feels that something is lacking in her life because she is alone. It's not because of the way other people treat her. She has friends and is included in social gatherings. People like her as a person. "If only Fran would be happy," they say. "It's so sad that she lets her disappointment about being single dominate her life."

What a contrast Fran is to my friend Virginia. I met Virginia because we share a common interest—angels. We had to work hard at our friendship because we lived about forty miles from each other and Virginia's husband was terminally ill. As much as possible she cared for him at home. When he was hospitalized, he wanted her to be near, so she was with him twenty-four hours a day. The nurses loved having her there because she was always cheerful and so appreciative of all they did.

Virginia was a constant help and support for her children and grandchildren. That was not easy, because they often laid their heartbreaking problems on her. She lived her faith and sought in every way to pass her Christian values on to her family. Her burdens were great, and Virginia faced them realistically.

Even when things were most difficult, I always looked forward to the times we could be together, for Virginia remained cheerful and had a positive attitude. "If I choose to be bitter," Virginia told me, "I just become a part of the problem. If I feel sorry for myself and focus on the problems, I end up being depressed, and the troubles just seem to grow. When I am carrying the heaviest burdens, that is when I need other people the most. If I continually complain, I drive them away. If I can be pleasant, they not only let me share my concerns but also give me relief as we talk about other interests." Virginia was not only pleasant; she gave me constant encouragement.

Years have passed and attractive Fran still seldom smiles. She remains unmarried. "She has so much to offer," one of her friends said recently, "and she wants to remarry so badly. I am certain she would have had a good marriage long ago if she had only faced life with a smile and a positive attitude."

In contrast, a year after Virginia's husband died, I attended her wedding. She was a radiant bride. The groom had known Virginia since they had attended school together as children. He had lost his wife a few years before. None of us were surprised that a good man would ask Virginia to marry him, for we all enjoyed being with her and knew she would be fun to live with. We also knew that, married or not, Virginia would have a fulfilling life, finding strength from God and sharing happiness with others along the way.

The person who accentuates the positive most often finds fulfillment.

Finding the Best in the Worst Places

Dana May Casperson was addressing the Victorian Tea Society. Dana May is perhaps the leading authority on tea in the United States. Of course tea had been served before the meeting, and during this social time Dana May had been meeting the members and listening as the members talked about their most recent visits to the tea houses in southern California.

Dana May began her talk by observing, "I have enjoyed meeting the members of this society who share my passion for tea. I listened intently as you spoke about the many places you have to go for tea in southern California. I must confess my surprise. I had expected to hear what was special about one tea house and what was delightful about another. Do you know what I did hear?—critics pointing out the faults of every tea room. The service at tea room A was not as good as it had been. The scones at tea room B were too hard and their lemon curd too sour. Tea room C had evidently allowed the tea to brew too long and it had become bitter."

"Now I recognize that you are experts when it comes to tea and its accoutrements," Dana May continued, "but in straining at the details you miss the real point. When you go for tea, go to enjoy the experience. Find the delightful. Don't look for things to criticize. Find those things you can take quiet pleasure in. Tea time is meant to be a joy. The true tea expert is one who knows how to enjoy the art of taking tea."

Right on! I thought. *That principle is true about more things than tea!*

The sweet old lady is one who has learned to go through life expecting to find enjoyment and good things. She goes to church looking for a blessing. Is it any wonder she is blessed, while others leave the same service complaining that the sermon was too long and the tenors in the choir were flat?

The sweet old lady has learned that we usually find what we look for in life. If we look for happiness, we can find it. If we look for problems, they will be there. If we search for what is depressing in the situation we are stuck with, we will discover plenty to spoil our day. If we seek out the benefits of even a bad situation, we will become aware of hidden blessings. We will find what we are looking for.

When I was a little girl, the book *Pollyanna* was popular. It is the fictional story of a young girl who never complained but always saw the bright side of everything. Whenever I would fret, my mother would say, "Be a Pollyanna and look on the bright side." But somehow that never helped. I thought that if Pollyanna was going through what I was going through, she would be unhappy too.

Thank God for Fleas?

Now I am an adult, and I have learned the wisdom of listening to those who have been through greater problems than I have faced. When I find myself in a discouraging situation, I often remember a lesson I learned from Corrie ten Boom. Corrie and her sister, Betsie, were prisoners in Ravensbruck, the dreaded Nazi concentration camp. They were assigned to Barracks 28, a filthy, smelly building. More than fourteen hundred prisoners were quartered in a space designed to hold four hundred people. To make matters worse, the barracks to which they were assigned was swarming with fleas. "Betsie, how can we live in such a place?" Corrie cried.

"Show us. Show us how," Betsie said. It was a prayer, not a reply to her sister. There was a moment of silence, then Betsie said excitedly, "God gave us the answer this morning. Take your Bible and reread the verses we shared this morning."

No guards were in sight, so Corrie turned to 1 Thessalonians and read: "Comfort the frightened, help the weak, be patient with everyone. See that none of you repays evil with evil, but always seek to do good to one another and to all . . ."

"That is exactly the message we need today in Ravensbruck. But go on," Betsie urged.

Corrie continued reading. "Rejoice always, pray constantly, give thanks in all circumstances; for this is the will of God in Christ Jesus—"

"There's our answer," Betsie exclaimed triumphantly. "God gave it to us this morning before we even asked him. 'Give thanks in all circumstances.' Let's do that right now."

Corrie stared around the dismal, overcrowded prison barracks. "What do we have to be thankful for?"

"Thank you, God, that we're still together," Betsie began. "And that we weren't searched before we came in here so we still have our Bible."

Corrie nodded in agreement.

"Thank you that we are packed so close in here so that many more women will hear about you." Betsie waited for her sister to join in the prayer.

"Oh, all right," Corrie heard herself saying. "Thank you for this overcrowded place, stuffed and jammed with people."

Betsie prayed on serenely, "And thank you, God, for the fleas . . ."

That was more than Corrie could agree with. "Sister, how can I be grateful for fleas?" she blurted out.

"It doesn't say 'in pleasant circumstances.' It says, 'Give thanks in all circumstances.' And in our circumstances there are thousands of fleas."

Corrie didn't argue the point as her sister gave thanks for the fleas, but in her own mind she was sure Betsie was wrong.

There was only one small light in the huge room in Barracks 28. Each night, as many of the women as possible would crowd together to hear Betsie and Corrie read from the Bible. They wondered why it was they had such freedom. Guards almost never entered Barracks 28.

One night, Corrie came home late from her work detail. She found her sister smiling, with a twinkle in her eye. "I just found out why we have had such freedom in this big room," Betsie said. "I heard the guards talking about why none of them would set foot inside our barracks. It's because the place is crawling with fleas!"

The two sisters joined hands and Corrie prayed, this time with enthusiasm and sincerity, "Thank you, Lord. Thank you especially for the fleas."

When I find myself complaining, I think of Corrie and her fleas. My situation is never as bad as the Ravensbruck prison, so I remind myself I can learn from her example. If she could find something good about fleas, I surely can find something good about the people and places I am stuck with. The clouds begin to lift and the day becomes brighter when I stop looking at my "fleas" and begin searching for what I can give thanks for.

What's Left?

One day as I was pouring out my troubles to a friend, she wisely said, "Marilynn, do you have a paper and pen handy? I want you to write something down that has been a great help to me." Here is the message she gave me: *Do not look at what you have lost. Look at what you have left.* "I've listened to your problems and my heart goes out to you because of your losses," she said sincerely. "If you continue to dwell on these losses, it will only add to your misery. Instead, tell me what you have left. You may have to look hard, but what can you be grateful for?"

It was hard at first. I was so discouraged I couldn't think of anything good to say, but with my friend's continued gentle urging, I began to find first one thing and then another. As I changed my focus, I found it easier to discover the many blessings that still remained. I realized the choice was mine. I could think only of my losses and wallow in sadness, or I could rejoice in all I had to be thankful for. I chose to be thankful, and like each person who has made that choice, I find my life is richer for it.

Try always to accentuate the positive, even if you must work hard to find the best in the worst places.

FOUR

You Can't Win If You Are Not in the Game

A sweet old lady is an active participant in life.
A grumpy old grouch lets life pass her by.

Henry Kissinger gave the commencement address to an Ivy League university. As Secretary of State, he had traveled the world and had been a part of many events that would shape history. The message he chose to give was drawn from his years of experience. It was the advice he felt these bright, young people graduating from a prestigious institution most needed to hear. His profound words of wisdom were, "You can't win if you are not in the game."

Henry Kissinger observed that life had simply seemed to pass by many of his former students and people he knew. In trying to understand why they had not found fulfillment, he discovered that it was not due to a lack of ability or training. It was because they had placed themselves on the sidelines. If the opportunity they dreamed of had not come easily, they became impatient and stopped trying. When problems came, they found it easier to drop out rather than to work through a difficult situation. Almost always, when an opening for the stepping-stone to their dream came, the chance was given to someone else—someone who had persisted. "You can't win if you're not in the game." We all need to take these words to heart.

A Wise Mother

If you stay in the game, you never know when something unexpectedly wonderful may happen. That was my experience with the whole realm of angels.

My interest in angels began when I was four years old. As a little girl in Chicago, I was afraid of the dark. Every night I would plead with my mother to stay with me, at least until I had fallen asleep. My mother tried everything to help. She read bedtime stories, told me Bible stories, sang to me and with me, but nothing seemed to help. One night she said, "Marilynn, I have a surprise for you." She read to me from Psalm 91:11: "For he shall give his angels charge over thee, to keep thee in all thy ways." She told me God loved me, and he had sent an angel to watch over me. Even though I couldn't see him, the angel was always with me, caring for me. Then she opened a brown paper bag and took out an angel figurine. I thought it was the most beautiful thing I had ever seen. She placed it on my dresser and said, "At night, when you are in bed, look at this angel and let it remind you that you are not alone. Remember there is a real angel that God has sent to watch over you." That night I slept soundly, comforted by the thought of my guardian angel.

As a young child, I began to collect angels. I would save my birthday money and my allowance then go to the dime-store and ask, "Please show me your angels."

The clerks would usually look at me and say, "Little girl, angels are just for Christmas. Come back at Christmas and we will have some angel ornaments."

"No, they're not just for Christmas," I would insist. "My guardian angel is always with me." The store clerks would exchange knowing looks, as if to say, "Poor little religious child," and they would say, "Just come back at Christmas."

In spite of the discouragement, my interest in angels persisted. I did come back at Christmas to add to my collection. Slowly my collection grew. I tried to learn all I could about angels.

An Angel on the Railroad Tracks

When I was a freshman in high school, my family moved from Chicago to Wheaton, Illinois. Since only a few weeks of the school term were left at Austin High School, I stayed with a friend in Chicago during the week and took the train to my new home in suburban Wheaton on the weekends. One Friday I learned that my favorite Sunday school teacher had cancer and had only a short time to live. She was young, in her early twenties. The news was devastating to me. I was in shock as I rode the Chicago, Aurora, and Elgin train to Wheaton. Death had never been a reality for me. It was something that happened to old people, and so far, to old people I did not really know. I had never had to deal with why bad things happened to good people. I tried to comfort myself with thoughts of heaven, but as the train made its thirty-mile journey, my sadness became more profound.

By habit I got off the westbound train at the College Street Station in Wheaton. I was so deeply depressed that I was completely unaware of my surroundings. Slowly, I began to cross the eastbound tracks on my way home when suddenly I heard the loud rumbling of a steam locomotive and the frightening blast of a train whistle. I was on the tracks, and the oncoming train was so close I could see the blue eyes and the terrified face of the engineer. But I was unable to move! I was so paralyzed with fear I could not even lift my foot. *I'm going to die,* I thought. *I'll be in heaven before my Sunday school teacher is.*

An instant before the train would have hit me, I was pushed. It was as if a giant hand had shoved me from behind, and I went flying off the tracks and fell on the cinders just below. Quickly I scrambled to my feet, grateful to be alive and wondering who the hero was who had saved my life.

No one was there! Not a person was in sight. There was a welling up in my heart as I realized I had been saved by my guardian angel. I hurried home, and when I met my mother, my words tumbled out as I told her of my close brush with death and my rescue by my guardian angel. My mother agreed it had to have been an angel. And as good mothers do, she took the opportunity to preach me a little sermon, "Marilynn, now that God has given you another chance, what are you going to do with your life?" The sermon really wasn't necessary, because once you have had an encounter with an angel, your life is never the same.

I shared the story with my mother, but I soon learned not to tell my friends. They thought angel stories were weird. I did not let their disbelief discourage me. I continued my interest in angels.

A Day to Remember

June 16, 1952, was one of the busiest days in my life. Surely it was one of the most unforgettable. That morning I graduated from Wheaton College. That evening I was married to Bill Webber, one of my college classmates. He became a pastor, and the people in our churches learned of my interest in angels. Through the years when they saw a representation of an angel, they would often think of me. Many times they would buy the angel and thoughtfully give it to me. Over the years my angel collection grew. Actually it grew very slowly, because few angels were to be found.

Enter Billy Graham

There were almost no books about angels. Then, in 1975, Billy Graham decided to preach a sermon about angels. He said he had never heard a sermon about angels. He looked in his library. He had no books on angels. He went to the Christian bookstores and discovered they did not have a single book on angels. There were many books on the occult, the Devil, and demons, but there were no books on angels. He went to the university library, but he searched in vain there as well. So Billy Graham decided to write a book about angels. The book, *Angels, God's Secret Agents* became a best-seller, and people began to talk about angels.

I began to receive calls from people who said, "Marilynn, Billy Graham's book has gotten people interested in angels.

Would you bring a few pieces from your collection and talk about angels at our next meeting?" I was delighted finally to be asked to share my passion. At first, many of the groups I talked to were often small, but I was gaining experience talking about my favorite subject. Surprisingly, people at these groups would share their testimony about angel experiences they had had. I began to collect these stories, never realizing they would be put into books that thousands of people would read. I loved what I was doing, and even though it did not seem to be important, I continued to study about angels and share what I had learned with whoever was interested.

My Interest Pays Off

I still was a frustrated angel collector. Few were to be found in the stores. My husband began to urge me to get a seller's license, go to the marts and gift shows, and search through the thousands of manufacturers and distributors. "Someone must be making angels," Bill told me. I began the first all-angel shop in the country, but when I talked to the manufacturers' representatives, they all told me the same thing I had heard since I was a little girl: "Angels are just for Christmas." Still, I persisted and tried to persuade them that angels would sell all year. I later heard that in company boardrooms from Los Angeles to New York they talked about the "Angel Lady from California" who said there was a growing interest in angels and that there would be a market for angel merchandise.

An Explosion of Interest in Angels

I wrote magazine articles on God's heavenly hosts, but they seemed to draw little attention. Still not discouraged, I wrote the story about Estella Vera, a woman in my hometown whose life had been changed because of an experience with an angel. After it was published in the October 1992 issue of *Guideposts* magazine, I received over eighty-five hundred letters from readers. I knew something new was happening, but I was not prepared for the surprise God had in store for me.

Since I was four years old I had pursued my interest in angels with little or no encouragement from others, simply trying to do whatever I could to increase the awareness of others in God's heavenly host. Now my personal angel collection had grown to more than thirty-five hundred pieces. My files were filled with true stories about angels working in lives today. Many of these accounts had come from the thousands who wrote me in response to the *Guideposts* story. I had tried to learn all I could about angels from a Christian perspective.

In 1992, David Briggs, the Religion Editor of the Associated Press, called. Tracking current trends, he had discovered an explosion of interest in angels. "I understand you are one of the experts on angels in the United States," he said.

"I am?" I replied. Once I was over the shock, I sent up an SOS prayer asking God's help in this impromptu interview. I explained I did not consider myself to be an expert. I did have a lifelong interest in the heavenly beings, had tried to learn all I could about them, and enjoyed writing and talking about them. "You open the Bible, and there's a rustle of angels," I heard myself saying. I had never used that expression before. David Briggs liked it, and "A Rustle of Angels" was used as the headline for an article about the growing interest in angels that appeared in newspapers across the country. The papers told my story and of my interest in the heavenly hosts through the years.

An intense interest in angels followed, and I found myself in the center of it. The *Ladies' Home Journal* called, asking if it could use my story and if I would help with their 1992 Christmas issue. *TIME* magazine called and interviewed me for an hour and a half for its cover story on angels. Soon it became almost commonplace to receive calls from radio, television, and the print media. Next came a contract for a book. We called it *A Rustle of Angels.* In 1995 the book was nominated for a Gold Medallion Award, and it received the print media award from the Excellence in Media Foundation. It sold over 300,000 copies in hardback, and my husband and I appeared on hundreds of radio and television shows.

All this happened only because I had stayed in the game through the years, even when there seemed to be no interest on the part of others. Looking back, I now see what I did not know before. God was not surprised by the explosion of interest in angels. He knew that much of the fascination with angels would happen outside the church. He had been preparing me to be at the center of the explosion of interest in angels to give the mainstream Christian and biblical perspective on angels. Little did I realize that my part was to keep on keeping on. You can't win if you are not in the game!

FIVE

Do Your Best and the Lord Will Bless

A sweet old lady does what she can with what she has. A grumpy old grouch quits if everything does not work out.

For seven years my husband was the administrator of a retirement home that was a part of the American Baptist Homes of the West. I was invited to his retirement dinner, which included a good-natured "roast" as his colleagues recalled several of his most embarrassing moments. Seated at our table that night was Kay Kallander, the administrator of the Plymouth Village Retirement Community in Redlands, California. As we reminisced about the past, Kay shared this remarkable story.

A Mission of Mercy

After a year of preparation, Kay was finally on her way. She was a nurse, and she had volunteered to spend her vacation using her professional skills on the mission field. The Trinity Baptist Church in Santa Monica had been working for a year to raise funds to send a team of four to Haiti. Joining Kay from California was Dr. Charles Wood, a dentist, and Kathleen Whitney, another nurse. They would meet Dr. Miranti, another dentist from New Jersey, in Haiti. Their mission was to give dental care to hundreds of people who had no access to a dentist.

On her way to the airport, Kay stopped at the hospital where she had been working on the cardiac ward. Kay had been assigned to a patient who was very interested in her coming mission trip and very touched by the work she was about to do. The patient was scheduled to go into surgery, and Kay wanted to give him some extra encouragement before she left. It was needed. The man understood the seriousness of his condition. He told Kay, "I'm just about to go into surgery, and I don't know whether I am going to come through this or not. I want you to take this envelope—I've put a little money in it—and take it to Haiti. It may be that when you are there you will discover some things you need that you hadn't anticipated, like aspirins or something."

The nurse objected, "I can't do that."

The patient persisted, "I absolutely insist."

"That is very thoughtful of you," Kay replied. "Thank you." She placed the envelope in her purse, assured the patient he would be in her prayers, and hurried to the airport.

The flight to Haiti was uneventful, but going through customs was a disaster. The group had to bring all their supplies and equipment with them, so they arrived with several large boxes. The customs officials confiscated all of Dr. Wood's expensive portable dental equipment and all the supplies they were carrying in—Lidocaine for anesthesia, dressing materials, surgical gloves, inoculation supplies, and even baby vitamins. Dr. Rick Miranti, the dentist from New Jersey, flew in with only one small backpack. The customs officials let him pass without checking it. Inside his backpack was one set of dental equipment and a small amount of Lidocaine. The four huddled in the airport waiting room, lifting their urgent prayers. They decided to leave the terminal and regroup outside.

Dr. Miranti did have his portable dental equipment, but he only had about fifty ampoules of the anesthetic Lidocaine.

Since some patients require more than one ampoule, it meant only a few patients could be helped.

A missionary had come to pick them up. On the way to his home, they shared their disappointment. For a year they had planned and prayed and worked so they could bring health and relief from pain to many. Now it seemed their trip would be in vain. The four were so discouraged that they considered packing up and returning home.

Instead, they decided to do what they could. They would open the clinic. The dentists would take turns using the one set of equipment. They would use the anesthetic as long as it lasted—probably an hour or two—then they would have to close the clinic.

In the morning they set up what had to be the world's smallest dental clinic. They were in the open air, except for a roof that sheltered them from the direct sun. There was one table. A dentist and a nurse would work as a team at each end of the table. A long line of hopeful patients patiently waited their turn. No one had the heart to turn them away. The dentists were experts and worked quickly. The nurses would prepare the patients, load a syringe with the anesthetic, and hand it to the dentist. The dentist would give the shot, then do the necessary procedures on the patient. When he was finished, he would pass the portable equipment to his colleague. There would be just enough time to sterilize equipment and do a preliminary examination of the next patient before the dental tools became available again.

Hours passed. Patients came, were treated, and left. Kay continued loading syringes from the limited supply of ampoules in her box. The supply never ran out.

At the end of a long day the weary team closed their clinic. "We must have treated over two hundred patients today," Dr. Wood observed. "That's a record for me."

"Thank God we never ran out of our anesthetic," Kay observed. "Where did the additional supplies come from? Kathleen, you must have kept replenishing my box."

"No, Kay," Kathleen replied. "I thought you were putting the ampoules in my box. It had to be one of the dentists, then." But neither of the dentists had found additional medicines. No one else could have come up with the needed supplies and placed them unnoticed at the nurses' makeshift station. The entire team recognized they had been a part of a miracle. In the New Testament, Christ had compassion on the multitude and had multiplied the loaves and the fishes until the need was met. This day, God in his mercy had kept the dental supplies from running out. They joined together in a prayer of thanksgiving. They had done what they could, and the Lord added what was needed.

Now they needed to decide what to do next. By the grace of God they had made it through one day, but should they presume on God and expect him to miraculously continue to multiply the anesthetic as long as they were there? Their expensive equipment and supplies had been wrongly impounded. They were sorely limited because so much of what they needed was locked away in customs. In addition to the portable dental equipment, they needed the collapsible dental chair. Designed by a student at the University of Southern California, it was lightweight, made of cardboard, but very sturdy and serviceable. The customs officials had said they would release the equipment and supplies, but only if a large sum of money would be paid. Before planning their mission of mercy, the group had reviewed the customs regulations, and they knew they were not required to pay this exorbitant amount.

The dentists and nurses decided to return to customs and try again. Rather than go as a group, they thought it wiser for each of them to try individually. It might be that one would find a sympathetic official and be able to negotiate a more favorable settlement.

Dr. Wood tried to appeal to the compassion of the customs officer. He explained they had come as volunteers to treat people who otherwise would have no dental care. They were offering their services for free. The customs officer would be doing a service to his people by releasing their equipment and supplies. His argument fell on deaf ears.

Kay was the only one who was able to make any progress. After some haggling, one customs official told her he would release all their equipment and supplies if she would pay him five hundred American dollars. Kay returned to the group to report. Five hundred dollars was much less than the amount demanded before, but this was an expense they had not anticipated, and it seemed impossible.

"An expense that wasn't anticipated." The words jogged something in Kay's memory. She told her group about the visit she had made to the hospital on the way to the airport and the envelope the friend had given for expenses that hadn't been anticipated. "He said it was for aspirins or something we might need," Kay explained. "It's probably only ten dollars or so." The envelope was still in her purse, unopened.

Kay opened the envelope and discovered it held five hundred dollars cash. Five hundred American dollars! Exactly the amount needed. Quietly they lifted a prayer of thanksgiving. The volunteer missionary team redeemed their equipment and supplies.

During the next few weeks they ministered with skill and Christian love to hundreds of patients. They set up their clinic in remote villages, sometimes hiking to their destination on mountain trails. Other times, they were located in a school building. Kay remembers working one day on the beach. The day was so hot it was oppressive, but for the Haitians patiently waiting in line, this was their only chance to have their dental work done. When Kay was covered with perspiration and felt she could not endure the intense heat any longer, her patients taught her to do as they did. She learned to wade into the ocean until she was covered with water, then walk out. She would return to work, soaking wet, and be cooled by natural evaporation.

They ministered to hundreds of people who otherwise would never have seen a dentist. It would have been reward enough for Kay to see the relief from pain and suffering they were able to give so many. "But what I will never forget," Kay Kallander told me, "was the day our supply of Lidocaine miraculously never ran out. I learned that day that when I do my best with what little I have and trust God for the rest, he will see me through. He always has. And I believe he always will for everyone who trusts him."

Never Give Up

I remember Kay's experience when I am tempted to give up and quit. Becoming discouraged is easy when something has gone wrong. Too often we do nothing because we can't do everything. How sad it would have been if Kay and her companions had packed up and gone home in disgust when their equipment and medications were confiscated. How much better to decide to treat the few patients they could and trust God for what would happen next.

President Theodore Roosevelt often repeated, "Do what you can with what you have where you are."

I was always inspired by the Willing Workers, a group of women in Springfield, Missouri, who met every Friday morning at the University Heights Baptist Church. These were women who were seventy, eighty, and ninety years old. They were noted for the beautiful quilts they made. They accomplished much besides quilting. This was their motto:

I am only one,
But still I am one.
I cannot do everything,
But still I can do something;
And because I cannot do everything
I will not refuse to do the something that I can do.

Edward Everett Hale

This book is about finding joy, meaning, and purpose each day you live. It is about a lifestyle that in time comes naturally to the woman who is maturing and growing wiser with each year. This lifestyle is not one of constant struggle. A woman who exercises regularly will feel better physically because she has followed a sensible fitness program. Even those exercises that took effort in the beginning become easy and even enjoyable as they are repeated daily. In the same way, a woman who commits to applying biblical principles to each situation will discover a peace and freedom as she approaches each day. Her priorities will be established.

Life may be unpredictable, but she knows she can count on the grace of God to help her as she faces each opportunity with a Christian spirit. She does not need to be able to do everything or know all the answers. She only needs to do her best and know that the Lord will bless.

SIX

Do What You Can

A sweet old lady works around her limitations.
A grumpy old grouch says, "I can't."

Janet Pillsbury, my sister-in-law, was faced with a dilemma. She was copresident of the Lupus Group of Maine. The members decided it was important to raise public awareness about Lupus. They also wanted to raise funds for the patient services the group was offering as well as research and treatment of the disease.

Other organizations had some dynamic members that could organize spirited events to meet these goals. But all the members of this group had Lupus, and one of the main symptoms of the disease is overwhelming fatigue. On a bad day, which can never be predicted, a person with Lupus is not able to do even simple chores. This group could not go on a walkathon, hold garage sales, car washes, or other typical fund-raisers that required strength and energy.

Janet decided to find what the group could do. She wanted it to be something the group could do itself because so often those with Lupus feel they are always asking someone else to do things for them. What could the Lupus group do wherein they would be the main participants?

"What do we do?" she asked herself. "What do we do well? What do we do a lot of? We rest! Why not have a rest-a-thon?" Excited, Janet called the executive board with her idea. A rest-a-thon would be something they could do themselves. It would highlight one aspect of the disease. Members of the group would ask neighbors, friends, and family to pledge an amount for each hour they rested on the day of the Lupus rest-a-thon. There would be no overhead, so any money raised would go directly to the cause. People were intrigued, and they were willing to help when they saw someone they knew who had the illness doing what he or she could.

"Where could we hold a day-long rest-a-thon?" one member asked.

"Let's choose a church," Janet laughingly replied. "What's more conducive to sleeping than a church pew?" They began a search for a church with padded pews that would be willing to host the rest-a-thon. They found a sympathetic Nazarene pastor who agreed to open his church from 8:30 A.M. to 4:30 P.M.

Resting eight hours at home is one thing. Sitting or lying on a church pew—even a padded pew—is quite another. The group would need to find activities to occupy their time. Janet began to network. She called and asked people to help provide program activities.

On the appointed day the Lupus Group of Maine filed into the church, bringing pillows and blankets.

Some were dressed in nightclothes, pajamas, and robes. All wore comfortable clothing. During the day some sat; others would lie on the padded pews. A woman with a beautiful voice came and sang lullabies to the group. A storyteller told several stories. A father dressed in pajamas and big slippers came with his two daughters to read bedtime stories. The host pastor was also an excellent writer, and he willingly read them several of his articles. Janet recruited a string quartet to play, and several instrumentalists and soloists rounded out the day. Just enough time was left to talk and support one another.

Supermarkets donated food for the fund-raiser, and some of the members brought things they had prepared, so lunch was a time of quiet celebration.

Members of the Maine Support Group live all over the state. For some it was too far to travel to the site. For others, their fatigue on the day of the rest-a-thon was too great for them even to come to the church to rest. From the beginning, it had been decided they could be full participants by resting at home.

The unusual activity was a natural for publicity. One radio news reporter began his coverage by saying, "I can't believe this. You've got to listen to this one ..." Then he went on to tell about the rest-a-thon. The event was covered in newspapers, on radio, and on TV.

In an extended television interview, Janet explained that more than a half-million people suffer from Lupus. It affects more people than either MS or muscular dystrophy but receives far less attention. This is unfortunate because many people with Lupus do not know the symptoms, so they do not seek help.

When the rest-a-thon was over, the group's goals had been met. Funds had been raised for patient support and research and treatment of the disease. Public awareness about Lupus had increased. Several people with Lupus had learned about the support group and had become members. Others asked for literature and informational tapes the group provides.

Best of all was what happened to the members themselves. Several found this to be a time of bonding. They were together long enough to discover another person, a fellow sufferer, with whom they could share their struggles on a deep and personal level. Some who were there, even young women, were fighting for their lives in the battle against Lupus. One was in her twenties with a child; another was in her thirties with three children. For them, the day was one of hope, finding resources to cope, and having fun. They did what they could, and it was successful.

Do What You Can

Those on their way to becoming sweet old ladies develop a lifestyle where they do what they can. They are learning you don't have to have everything perfect to begin. They stop making excuses—you know the common ones! I've never done this before. I don't know how. I don't have enough ability. I don't have time to do it right. I might fail. I might make a fool of myself. I don't have the right tools. I can't afford it.

Perhaps the most crippling excuse of all is this: Someone else can do it better than I. Of course they can! Few of us are world class in our efforts. If you enjoy playing the piano, don't stop because you can't play as well as Van Cliburn (or Roger Williams or Dino or whomever you consider to be the best). Enjoy using the talent you have. Be honest, though. You're not really comparing yourself to these concert pianists, are you? Isn't it really with Mrs. Jones, who is also in your group? Why place yourself in competition with her and judge yourself as inferior? How much better to do what you can and enjoy doing it, realizing that most people probably can't tell much difference between your playing and that of Mrs. Jones.

Bruce Larson has said, "If something is worth doing, it is worth doing poorly." This assumes that under the given circumstances you are not able to do the needed thing well. If it needs to be done, getting it done even imperfectly is better than leaving it undone. That you are not gifted with words is no excuse not to write a letter to your family. You may not be the best cook, but it is better to prepare the foods you can cook rather than to go hungry. You may not be the hostess with the mostest, but you will be richer if you do invite friends to your home. You may not have a solo voice, but you could be a contribution to your church choir. According to the great choral director, Robert Shaw, the best choirs are made up of ordinary voices.

A Slow Learner

Two years ago I wasn't practicing what I am preaching here. The manuscript for our book, *A Rustle of Angels*, was almost due. The research, fact checking, and writing of this book about God's angels was a time-consuming task, and it seemed everything else in my life also had a deadline. "It is so overwhelming," I confided to a friend, "that I feel like I'm literally being buried under all the good things I have to do."

I will never forget her advice. "Do your best. Leave the rest. Angels do no more."

Suddenly it put things in perspective for me. The major problem was my worry about the expectations I had placed on myself. If the angels did their best and were content to leave it at that, why couldn't I? I began to do only what I could. Not everything was done that in my worries I felt needed to be done, but when I stopped being drained and fearful about my workload, I was able to accomplish more. The truly important projects were completed, and having done my best I had no need to feel guilty.

Sometimes I forget. When I do, my husband points to a sampler cross-stitched by our daughter-in-law, Susan. She made it after I had shared with her the struggle I described above. In burgundy letters on a beige background it says, *Do your best. Leave the rest. Angels do no more.*

Learn to Adjust to Change

I met Marilyn Henderson in a psychology class at Wheaton College. Through the years we have remained good friends. Marilyn's husband, Walter, is a prince of a man. He was a physicist, and his field was the use of radio active isotopes in medicine. When Walter's eyesight began to fail, he tried various medical treatments. It was a difficult time. Each new procedure offered hope; when it was not successful, disappointment would follow. It became increasingly difficult for Walter to do his work. Finally, because of his blindness, he found it necessary to stop working and go on disability.

He enjoys being a grandfather. When a little one climbs on his lap and asks, "Grandpa, read to me," Walter explains that his eyes are broken and has the child describe the pictures to him. He works with the grandchildren on their science projects. There is much he cannot do, but his life is guided by the decision to give his best effort to what he can do.

Now, nine years after losing his sight, Walter is able to tell light from darkness, be aware of some shapes, and detect movement. His greatest disappointment is that he has only been able to see one of his six grandchildren. The inability to enjoy photographs is also difficult. Blindness is a major handicap. When I asked Walter what the advantages were of not being sighted, he laughed and replied, "I can't think of a single one."

His blindness is not a problem when we are together. What does impress us is to see Walter doing what he can. We do not feel that we are with a handicapped person. We admire him for being capable and willing to adjust to what cannot be changed. He still is an engaging dinner partner. It's just a normal part of the table talk for his wife to give him a few hints (the peas are on the plate at three o'clock and the mashed potatoes are at nine o'clock). Walter shares in the conversation. When it turns to news and current events, he is the most knowledgeable one at the table. The magazines he "reads" on his talking book have given him more depth than what I glean from the nightly newscasts. We turn to him for financial advice because he keeps up on the latest developments. When he attends seminars on subjects such as living trusts, he asks permission to record them since he cannot see to take notes.

Walter leads the program activities for the blind support group. Newcomers to the group are often struggling with the adjustment necessary to cope with failing eyesight or complete blindness. Walter is sympathetic. He has experienced it all. He knows the disappointment of losing one's sight and the difficulties in adjusting to life. He shares with them the resources they can draw on: the many books and magazines on tape without charge, aids and services available and how to access them, and agencies that will help with adjustment.

Walter offers hope. From his own experience he shares ways to accomplish routine tasks (don't try to put the toothpaste on a brush you cannot see—put the toothpaste on your teeth). He tells them how he continues to be quite independent around the house. His wife helps him, and in return he helps her by doing the laundry (he can feel the toothpicks glued to the dial), vacuuming the carpets, and mopping the floors. (His wife, Marilyn, sweeps them first.)

He tells the support group how important it is to get out of the house. Each week he attends a men's breakfast that his church sponsors at a local restaurant. He and his wife attend Elderhostels together. "We had a great experience at one in Hawaii," he told me. "The Elderhostel is an affordable way to combine learning and new experiences in a setting a blind person can handle."

It is Walter's great joy to see a blind person move from despair to a healthy adjustment and joy of living. Not all do, however. Some retreat from life and become despondent. A few choose suicide.

"What makes the difference?" I asked Walter.

"For me, it has been my faith in Jesus Christ and the love and support of my family," he answered without hesitation. "The joy I find in living is well worth any effort I make."

"Another factor I have found," he went on, "is the willingness to do what you can. Instead of brooding on what you cannot do, find ways to do what you can.

"What I find sad is the support group that meets in a home for the blind. You would expect the residents there to take advantage of the encouragement they can find from others who have a similar problem. Not one attends, however. They consider their lot to be hopeless, and choose instead to be completely dependent."

When a woman in their church lost her sight, Marilyn and Walter were there to help. They would stop on their way to church and give Rose a ride. The woman appreciated what they were doing. One Sunday Walter said, "Let me show you how you can go to church by yourself whenever you wish." Rose's home was only about three blocks from the church, so Walter had his wife drop him off. While Marilyn drove the car to the church, Walter demonstrated how a blind person could safely make the short walk. "I guess you could call it 'the blind leading the blind,'" Walter chuckled. Rose's adjustment to life will depend a great deal on her willingness to be as independent as possible, to do what she can.

"I have time to reflect," Walter told me, "and I believe it is not only true for those who are blind but for everyone. Our adjustment to life depends not on the obstacles we face but on our willingness to do what we can."

Nothing Too Small

Too often we do nothing because we cannot do anything big or important. Remember the little Dutch boy? He discovered a small hole in the dike. He knew that if nothing were done, the hole would become bigger and bigger until the dike would break, flooding his entire town. He was just a little lad. He couldn't do much, but he did what he could. He put his finger in the hole and stopped the water from coming in until help arrived. Do you remember the name of the boy? That's not important. We remember the story because it reminds us that so much—in fact, sometimes everything—depends on a small act done by someone behind the scene. Often these people go unnoticed and unrecognized, yet they are the real heroes.

Where do you meet the nicest people? I have discovered one place to look. My schedule as a speaker has taken me to some of the largest and some of the smallest churches and hundreds in between. When I arrive, I am usually met by the leaders, the movers and shakers, the people who preside over the meetings. I have met some wonderful women that way who have become lasting friends.

When I have completed the protocol of meeting leaders, when I have tended to the necessary details of the meeting, such as which microphone to use, then I love to slip into the kitchen. Sometimes I encounter a mess sergeant who has efficiently organized the refreshments or banquet. I know that later she will be recognized for her needed service. Usually I will find one or sometimes two or three women cheerfully but quietly working behind the scenes. When I start a conversation with them, I often discover the faithful, true-blue individuals who are a delight to be with. They are the giving people. Although they are often taken for granted, that doesn't matter to them. They know their service is important to their organization, and their joy is in seeing the conversation, the laughter, the fellowship that results from their tasks. You can meet the nicest people in a church kitchen.

I have met many people who believed they were too important for little acts of service. Of course, they never expressed it that way. Rather, they spoke of the importance of delegating work to others. Delegating is important; no one should try to do everything herself. We need to be careful not to attempt to do more than one person can do. But we should never be above doing the small chores that serve a purpose but receive no recognition.

I have discovered many wonderful women who are among the busiest people in the world. They have important responsibilities, yet it is not unusual to find them giving a helping hand when needed.

My husband pastored a church across the street from Southwest Missouri State University. One of the active church leaders and volunteers, E. Howard Matthews, was also one of the busiest professors on campus, dividing his time among teaching, administration, and work with the foreign students. One Sunday morning it snowed. Our church had a contract with a company to plow the parking lots and sidewalks around our church, but the wind had been blowing and snow had drifted across one of the entrances to the sanctuary. Dr. Matthews, seeing the need, took a shovel and cleared a path; then with a broom he swept the sidewalk clean. One of the freshman university students, coming to worship for the first time, was surprised to see his professor shoveling the snow. Later he was heard telling another student, "Did you know that our professor, Dr. Matthews, moonlights? I saw him working as a custodian at the church. He was shoveling the snow this morning."

"He wasn't moonlighting," his fraternity brother replied. "When you get to know him, you'll discover he's like that. He always pitches in and helps wherever needed."

The Most Important Work

My friend Stella was one of the sweetest old ladies I have ever met. Throughout her life she had been active, not only as a leader but also in those quiet acts of service in her church and for the people around her. After a lifetime of activity, Stella's health finally failed. I visited her in the nursing home. She was too weak to leave her bed. She greeted me with a smile and asked me to bring her up to date about the people and projects she loved.

"It must be hard for you to be confined to bed," I sympathized with her. "After being so active for so many years, it must be especially difficult to be in a position where there is nothing you can do."

"Marilynn," she replied, "it's true I don't like to be in bed all day, but it's not true that there is nothing I can do. I am doing the most important work in the world."

"And what is that?" I asked.

"Prayer," Stella replied. "Prayer is the most important work in the world."

Do What You Can

The woman on her way to becoming a sweet old lady makes it her practice to do what she can. Sometimes this places her in a position of leadership. Often she works quietly behind the scenes without recognition. Nothing is beneath her. No job is too small. She accepts her limitations but finds creative ways of accomplishing tasks in spite of them. The simple commitment to do what she can makes an important difference in her life and the lives of those around her.

SEVEN

Wait Expectantly

A sweet old lady has learned to wait expectantly. A grumpy old grouch is impatient.

It was a time of decision. My husband had completed four years of college and three years of seminary. During this time he had served on the staff of two large churches in Chicago, but our dream had always been that Bill would be the pastor of his own church. Now he had been invited to meet with a church and preach a trial sermon. Following the Sunday morning service would be a time when the congregation could ask the prospective pastor any questions they wished about his theology, his style of ministry, and his personal life. On the following Wednesday they would vote to extend a call. If they voted yes, we could either accept or decline the call to be the pastor of the church.

We had never heard of Hutsonville. It was a small town in southern Illinois. So small, in fact, it wasn't even on some maps. The sign at the city limits boasted a population of five hundred, a claim only strangers passing through took seriously.

Saturday we met with the church board for a time of questions and answers. We were drawn to these friendly people, and we found the church building to be attractive and in good repair. We thought the parsonage next to the church was attractive. One of the trustees told us he owned the house next door, which he used as a rental property. "That's good news," he told us. "I'll be able to see that you always have good neighbors."

Saturday night was spent in the home of the Herb and Pauline Woods, leaders in the church. Before breakfast Sunday morning, Pauline said, "Parson, I have a story I want to tell you. There was once a preacher who came to preach a trial sermon in a church. He stayed overnight in the home of one of the deacons. Sunday morning the deacon's wife prepared a big, special breakfast for the visiting clergy. When the minister came to the table, he didn't touch his food, explaining, 'I never eat before I preach.' Following the church service, the visiting pastor was shaking hands with the parishioners at the door. The deacon's wife looked him in the eye and said, 'Preacher, you might just as well have et.'"

Needless to say, my husband ate a hearty breakfast that morning.

There were sixty-seven people in church for the morning worship service. Bill preached a fine sermon, and the following Wednesday night Carl McCain, the chairman of the church board, called to say the church had voted unanimously to call Bill to be their pastor. We accepted the call.

On Bill's first Sunday as pastor, we were disappointed to find only thirty-five people in the morning worship service. Ped Huffman explained, "This is our usual attendance."

"But when we were here a few weeks ago, the attendance was sixty-seven. What has made the difference?" Bill asked.

A slow smile spread over Ped Huffman's face as he explained, "The Methodist church in town has services every other Sunday. When the Methodists heard that the Baptists were trying to get a pastor, they came to our church that Sunday to help us out." It worked. We were committed. It took a year, a lot of work, and prayer before attendance reached sixty-seven again.

A Death Threat

Our first visitor in the parsonage was the man who had owned the house next door. "I sold the house," he told us. "An old couple bought it. The wife doesn't think outsiders have any right to move into our town. She has been threatening to kill you. She has a gun. I thought you ought to know."

The next day I caught the first glimpse of our new neighbors. They *were* old. I was in my mid-twenties, and they looked ancient to me. The wife's face was weathered and wrinkled. His hair was thin, and his teeth were missing. Once the two of them were hanging the wash on the clothesline in their backyard. The old woman glared at me, grabbed her husband by the arm, and dragged him into their house. I had seen the hatred in her eyes. Was she going to get her gun? Hastily I retreated into my kitchen, where I told my husband my fears.

What should we do? It didn't seem right for us to leave before we had begun our ministry. Besides, being right out of seminary, we couldn't afford the moving expenses and we had nowhere to go. If we quit before we began, would another church take the risk to call us? Although the threat of death was frightening to us, we were young and idealistic. We decided to pray, to trust God for our safety, and to try to win the friendship of our neighbors. *A lot of people don't like preachers,* I thought, *especially for neighbors. That's probably their problem.* We did not tell our parents.

In the weeks that followed, we prayed that God would change the hearts of the couple next door. We looked for the opportunity to talk with them, but it never came. At times we did have a chance to smile at them, but all we received in return was a fierce frown that seemed to say, "Drop dead."

As time passed and I tried to gather clues about Mrs. T's problem, I noticed something interesting. If the neighbors were in their backyard and my husband went outside, they would ignore him. They would not respond to his friendly greeting, but they would go about their business—usually hanging up the wash—as if he were not there. But if I came out, Mrs. T would immediately grab Mr. T and drag him into the house. Her strongest feelings of hatred were clearly against me.

It hurt. I had never had an enemy who publicly threatened to kill me. I was the pastor's wife, and I knew that people expected me to return love for hate and find ways to win her friendship. I had discovered there were no secrets in this small town. I was convinced everyone knew how this neighbor hated me. Were they criticizing the new minister's wife because she couldn't make friends with her next-door neighbor?

I shared my concern with one of the older women in the church. "It seems I'm the one she hates," I confided. "I can't imagine why."

"Child, haven't you figured that one out?" her eyes twinkled merrily. "Everyone else in town has."

"No," I answered, a little irritated that she found anything humorous about something so painful to me. "She never even gives me a chance to talk to her, let alone ask what the problem is."

"Why, honey, that senile, old lady is afraid you are going to try to steal her husband!"

"But he's ancient! He's over eighty, and I'm only twenty-five," I objected. It didn't make sense. But suddenly I realized it didn't have to make sense. With my college degree and trying to be so "professional," I had been looking for a rational explanation while the rest of the town recognized her senility. When my neighbor lady heard that a "nice young minister and his wife" were moving in next door, that was enough for her unreasonable jealousy to turn into hatred directed toward the newcomer she saw as a possible rival. That's why she would drag the old man into the house the minute I set foot out of the door. For a moment I stood there, stunned. Then we both began to laugh.

I found relief knowing the rest of the town was not judging me. Still, it was painful to encounter such hostility from the woman next door, and my Bible taught me to love my enemies. I determined to pray and to find ways to overcome her dislike for me, to overcome evil with good. It seemed impossible when she would not even allow me to talk to her. I formulated a strategy. I would smile at her but not at her husband, since she would construe that as my flirting with him. I would speak a cheery hello, even though I knew it would be ignored. I would never give any sign of being irritated or upset because of the way she treated me.

I began to see our brief encounters as a challenge. I continued for over a year without seeing any perceptible change in her. It made a real difference to me, however. Living next to a spiteful neighbor no longer upset me.

Still, I wished for a positive resolution. It was not realistic to hope we would become close friends, but I longed to find some way to end her hostility. I knew it was hurting her. I had tried everything. Nothing had worked. I kept praying, but I admit to becoming somewhat impatient.

I read my Bible and listened to my young husband's first sermons. It seemed the Lord was telling me to be positive but patient. I was baffled. How could things ever get better?

God Works in Mysterious Ways

Our first baby was born. The women of the church gave a baby shower for our new baby girl that was absolutely overwhelming. I was certain that it was an answer to prayer that our daughter was born whole and healthy. We named her Sharon Linnea. She was showered with love by all the women in our small church, and our little girl grew up believing that everyone she met was a friend.

Sharon took her first steps at nine months. Once she began walking, there was no stopping her. She was filled with curiosity and a sense of adventure. One beautiful April day when my back was turned for an instant, Sharon headed out of our front door as fast as her little legs would carry her. In a few seconds I realized she was gone, and I rushed to the door. I saw our one-year-old had crossed our front lawn and was heading for our neighbor's front porch, where Mrs. T was sitting. When she was almost there, little Sharon lost her balance and was about to fall when old Mrs. T leapt out of her chair and caught the child before she could fall. Mrs. T held her close for a moment. Sharon smiled up at her, a warm thank-you smile for saving her from a fall. It was also the smile of a child expecting to be loved. When I approached, Mrs. T handed me my little girl. It was the first time I had seen our neighbor smile.

The next time we went out, Mrs. T was on her porch, rocking. Sharon waved to her. Taking my cue from my daughter, I waved, too. Mrs. T waved back. It was only a wave, but to me it was a giant breakthrough. The barrier with our neighbor had been broken. God had answered my prayer in a way I never would have expected. The next day we waved again. Soon we were exchanging greetings. I stopped wondering if Mrs. T would use her gun. I had learned to wait expectantly. I had discovered that God would work in his own way and in his own time.

God Is Always at Work

Years later, when I face what seems to be an impossible situation, I look back and remember how troubled I was that I was not able to find a solution to the hatred of my neighbor. I recall that God answered my prayers in a most unexpected way—by sending me a baby. Now I can see the value of the lessons I learned living next to a woman who had threatened to kill me. When I am tempted to be impatient that problems are not solved my way as quickly as I want, I remember that God is always at work in my life, just as he was in that little town in southern Illinois.

Lord, teach me always to wait expectantly.

EIGHT

Keep Doing What Is Needed

A sweet old lady keeps doing what is needed. A grumpy old grouch gives up easily.

The good news? Joan Anderson had five young children, including a new baby. The bad news? The house needed repairs. Where could the money be found? Joan decided it was up to her to find a way to supplement her husband's income. But what could she do with a houseful of children?

This wasn't the time to launch a career, Joan thought, but she needed to do something until she was able to find a job a busy mother could do. What did she have to work with? A growing family and a sense of humor. How could she stay at home with four—soon to be five—children and earn some money? Why not try writing? She tried and discovered a market for her articles on family humor.

Joan began to branch out to serious topics, mostly about the home and family. *Sometime in the future,* she thought, *there will come the chance for me to find that job.* While she was waiting, Joan did what she could. She continued to write. She wrote a book. It was published, so she wrote another, then another, until she had written seven. They were practical books about the family or how to begin a business in your home. From the publisher's point of view, they were successful, because they sold out their first printings. The books did not earn a great amount of money, but the royalty checks were a welcome addition to the family budget. Occasionally there would be a book club sale. It was just enough to make Joan think, *I guess I am a writer*, but her writing was always a means to something else. She did not look on it as a career; and she certainly did not consider that this was God's plan for her life. It was always a temporary thing, but while she waited for the right opportunity to come along, she did what she could.

When her youngest started school, Joan saw this as the opportunity to get a regular job with a paycheck every Friday. Every time she was about to begin a job search, an editor would call and ask her to take an assignment. The project would sound interesting, it would take only about a month, and Joan's creative juices would begin to flow again. It was always a temporary thing to raise funds because the children needed braces, the house needed new plumbing, or bills needed to be paid. Writing is often frustrating, but for Joan it needed to be done, so she just did it.

As the years passed, Joan became an established writer. Editors of some major magazines would count on her for well-written articles that would be submitted on time. Readers of the *Marriage and Family* magazine came to know her children as she wrote articles on the family. She distilled the lessons she learned about marriage for *Modern Bride* and other magazines. Still she was unaware that this was really a "calling" for her. She felt that God had a plan for her but did not see this as a part of the plan. When she had three children in college at the same time, she thought it important to earn what she could. She was merely being faithful in doing what needed to be done, unaware that all the while God was preparing her for something more. So Joan continued to write for ten years.

The Christmas Angel

It was past midnight on December 24, 1983. Her son Tim was driving home to Chicago for Christmas. Two friends, Don and Jim, were with him, and they had planned to drive straight through from Connecticut to Illinois. The first stop had been Fort Wayne, Indiana, where they had dropped Don at his family home. Although the roads were covered with snow, the windchill factor was at a record eighty degrees below zero, and the radio was broadcasting warnings telling everyone to stay off the roads, the two young men decided to complete the last four hours of their journey so they could be with their families on Christmas Day.

Heading for the Indiana Turnpike, Tim and Jim had traveled a few miles on a rural access road when suddenly their car's engine stopped. The road was deserted and not a farmhouse was in sight. The weather bulletins on the radio had bluntly stated that under these conditions any exposed skin would freeze in less than a minute. Quickly their car was becoming cold, but Tim and Jim knew that if they left their car, the temperature would kill them in a matter of minutes. They also knew they could not expect help to come. Not only was this a deserted country road, but it was after midnight on Christmas Eve, and others would have heeded the warnings to stay inside.

Even after repeated efforts, the car refused to start. "Well, God," Tim prayed, "you're the only one who can help us now." Minute by minute the cold grew more intense. Suddenly, headlights flashed from a truck behind the car. Tim was puzzled. How could a large tow truck approach without making a sound? Why hadn't they seen its headlights as it approached? A man, almost fully covered with a fur parka, hood, and gloves was knocking at their window. "Need to be towed?" he asked.

"Yes! Oh, yes, thanks!" Tim replied. The driver pulled the truck around the car and made the necessary connections. Jim and Tim asked him to bring them to a garage if one was open. If not, they asked to be towed back to Don's house.

They passed two locked service stations. They paused at one long enough to call Don and alert him that they were returning. The tow truck driver had not asked directions but had no difficulty locating the right cul-de-sac and without hesitation, stopped in front of Don's house. Don was waiting for them at the door as Tim and Jim rushed through the cold to meet him. "I'll need to borrow some money to pay the tow truck driver," Tim said.

"What tow truck?" Don asked. Tim and Jim turned. There was no truck. There had been no time for the driver to release the chains. They had heard no sound of the car's being uncoupled in the silent night, the tow truck door closing, or the chug of the truck driving away. There were no taillights disappearing in the distance. Tim's car was parked at the curb, but only one set of tire prints stood in the new snow, and they belonged to Tim's car. There were no truck tire prints anywhere.

What happened on that record-breaking cold night? Who was the mysterious driver that appeared from nowhere, did not wait to be paid or even thanked, and disappeared with his truck without leaving a trace? Tim Anderson is certain it was an angel.

A Mother's Quest

Joan, his mother, was overjoyed to hear that her son was safe, and she was thankful to God for his mysterious rescue. Like Mary in the Christmas story long ago, she kept all these things and pondered them in her heart. She was profoundly moved by the miracle, and it led her to go deeper in her spiritual life. She joined a prayer group and a Bible study group. Joan found herself asking, *What does this all mean? What does God want?* Looking back now, she can see that God was preparing her for what was to come.

At this same time, people began to share spiritual things with Joan. Over dinner in Sacramento, a person unburdened herself. Joan found the Holy Spirit giving her the wisdom to say what was needed. People would sit next to her in an airport and begin to talk. On a flight over Kansas, a seatmate turned to her and said, "Excuse me, but I feel I have to tell you something." The woman went on to share a thrilling experience of how God had ministered to her through an angel. Joan was amazed at how often she was hearing accounts of angels at work. As she pondered on her son Tim's miracle and the angel stories that kept coming to her, Joan became aware that God wanted her to do something.

With some trepidation Joan rented a post office box. She wrote to the magazines where readers would recognize her byline and asked them to publish this letter: *I am looking for people who believe they may have met an angel. I am not talking about human beings who, because of kindly deeds, might rightfully be called "angels." I am talking about spirits who appeared in human form to give some kind of help. Please write to me at this box number . . .*

Would the editors think she had become weird and stop accepting her manuscripts? Would any magazines print her letter? Would anyone respond? They did. It was overwhelming. Joan emptied the post office box and filled a grocery bag with the letters. A few days later her mother had outpatient surgery, so Joan and her sister spent most of the day in the waiting room. They opened the letters and found themselves laughing and crying as they read. So many people wrote, telling how they had found God's love and care through the ministry of angels. Joan's sister told her, "I don't know how this will come together, but you're going to have to write a book about angels."

Joan began the book in early 1990. She felt the book would be another "also ran." As far as she knew, there was a limited interest in angels. She had no idea that there soon would be an explosion of interest in angels in the world. She felt the book should not be released by a Christian publisher but by a secular publisher for broader exposure. Joan's track record with mainstream book publishers was not outstanding. Her books had each sold out their first printing of around five thousand, which was considered successful in the industry. That was not enough to make an acquisitions editor eager to take a chance on a new book, especially a book on angels, when there seemed to be so little interest in the subject. She knew that each year hundreds of thousands of manuscripts are submitted to publishers and only a few are published. There was no guarantee that if Joan wrote an angel book that it would ever be published. She could easily become discouraged and quit. Instead, she decided to just do it.

Joan began by writing Tim's story and submitting it to *Reader's Digest.* If it were published in their Christmas 1990 issue, Joan could take the tear sheet to the mainstream book publishers as a way of gaining their interest in the book. The *Reader's Digest* editor cried when she read the article. She loved it, went through all the channels, and told Joan it was definitely in. Before *Reader's Digest* prints any article, a professional fact checker verifies every detail. The fact checker talked to everyone involved in Tim's story and found all things were just as Joan had written in the story—with one exception. He was not able to talk to the tow truck driver. No such person could be found working at the local towing companies. "Of course not," Joan explained. "The driver had to be an angel." Because the fact checker could not talk to the angel, *Reader's Digest* would not run the story! Joan was given the news in October 1990. It was too late to submit the story to another magazine. The approval then rejection by the *Digest* had put her a year behind in marketing the book. Joan realized that it would be difficult, perhaps impossible, to interest a publisher in the book now. It would have been easy to quit, but she felt it was the right thing to do, and she kept on working.

Doing Lunch on the Telephone

It was a cold, dreary winter day in February when Joan's friend, Barbara Brett, called. She was going to be in Chicago on business and asked if it would be possible for the two of them to do lunch. When Joan told her she was not available on those dates, Barbara replied, "Why don't we have lunch right now over the telephone?"

In past years Barbara had been a magazine editor who had worked with Joan on many articles. Now she was vice president of a book publishing company but one that would never publish a book about angels. "What's going on in your life?" Barbara asked. Joan confided her disappointment about the *Reader's Digest* rejection because the fact checker could not locate Tim's angel. As Joan talked about her angel book in progress, Barbara became strangely silent. *I wonder if she believes in angels,* Joan thought. *Maybe she thinks I've flipped out.*

A few days later Barbara called again. She explained that for some time she and a partner had planned to begin a new book publishing company. Everything was ready except they needed a special manuscript to become their first book. They had both agreed they would recognize it when it came. "Joan," Barbara said, "Your angel book is just what we are looking for. We'll call it *Where Angels Walk.*"

Joan worked to finish the manuscript. In the fall of 1991 a friend sent Joan a clipping about *A Book of Angels* by Sophy Burnham. Joan was surprised to learn there was another angel book. Two or three times before, Joan had been working on a book and had lost out because another book on the same subject had come out before, hers was finished. Would she be scooped again? Standing on the porch where she had opened the mail, Joan didn't know whether to be happy or sad, and she said, "God, what do you think?" An inner voice that she recognized as God speaking answered, *I have plenty of angels for everyone.*

Joan took this as a signal to her that meant, *You are on this path: Go! Don't worry at all but keep your eyes on the prize. Don't worry about what anyone else is doing. Don't give up— just do it.*

The book came off the presses in June 1992, but since it was the first book from a new publisher, bookstores were not willing to stock it. Joan could have become discouraged and quit, and it would have all ended there.

But Joan found a company with an 800 number that would fill telephone orders for her book. They took a small supply on consignment and agreed to fill retail orders for individual customers or wholesale orders for bookstores. But how could Joan get individuals or stores to order her book?

Joan began to call radio stations and offer to give an interview on her latest book. They would ask the subject of the book, and when they learned it was about angels they would reply, "We're not a religious station." Joan would tell them, "This is not a religious book—not in the sense you are talking about." There would be a long silence, excuses given, and a polite refusal. It would have been easy to quit, to give up on the subject of angels and her book, but she did not. Instead she looked for a new approach.

Then, one day Joan noticed an article in the *Wall Street Journal* stating there was an explosion of interest in angels. Following up on that article, Joan began to call the radio talk show hosts in small cities. She would say, "While we are talking, let me fax you this article from the *Wall Street Journal*." When announcers saw that the *Wall Street Journal* called angels a current trend, they would decide to do an interview with Joan.

Next, Joan called all the bookstores in town and told them she was going to be on the local radio station promoting her book. Joan learned quickly that most bookstores would not order her book simply because of a local interview. But Joan refused to quit. Instead, she told bookstore managers she understood, but she wanted to alert them that there would be some people coming in saying, "I heard some lady on the radio talking about a book on angels. I don't remember the title, but can you get it for me?" Joan told bookstore managers the title is *Where Angels Walk* and gave the 800 number where it could be ordered.

Seeking a wider audience, Joan repeatedly sent information to the Associated Press, suggesting that it do a story on the growing interest in angels. Always she received no response. When the Associated Press did do an article, it made no mention of Joan and her book. It was discouraging, but Joan did not quit.

The Faith Daniels television show called some of the people in the newspaper articles, and they told the producer about Joan and her book. Joan was invited to be on a TV talk show about angels. The producers of the Joan Rivers show were watching and contacted Joan. "Would Joan Anderson be willing to come on our show?" they asked.

"Why did you choose me?" she inquired.

"You sounded believable," came the answer, "and we thought you looked like a midwestern housewife."

"I *am* a midwestern housewife," Joan replied.

The show was aired on December 8, 1992, and Joan Rivers held up *Where Angels Walk* and said, "This is a wonderful book. People should give this as a Christmas gift." Orders for 15,000 books poured in. The book was on its way. *Where Angels Walk* went on the *Publishers Weekly* best-selling religious and inspirational list in January 1993. Then the book went on the *New York Times* best-seller list, where it remained a year. Today it has sold more than one and a half million copies.

Joan remembers how the first thousand were sold, one book at a time, out of the trunk of her car. Later she asked one of her prayer partners, "If God was going to give me a best-seller, why didn't he do it earlier?"

Her friend replied, "So that you could see and understand that it was God's doing, not yours."

Joan remembered how in February 1992 she had made a new commitment placing God first in her life before all other things, including her writing. Since that time she always spent time in prayer before she ever turned on her computer to write, no matter how pressing the deadlines. She remembered how at that time she read in Joel, "I will repay you for the years the locusts have eaten" (Joel 2:25). It seemed to Joan that this was a promise God meant for her as well. *That first part fits me exactly*, Joan thought. *I feel as though swarms of locusts have just picked me clean through the years. I have stayed at home raising my family, writing articles on child care, and now I feel empty. I have nothing more to give.* It was then Joan realized she could not do it herself—that whatever happened with the book she was writing had to be of God. Now she praises God that he has not only blessed others through her but has heaped blessings on her as well.

"Never give up," Joan counsels. "All things are possible with God."

Joan's story illustrates the principles of a sweet old lady in the making. First, do what is necessary. To help pay the bills while she cared for her young family, Joan began to write magazine articles and books. Second, do what you think is God's call. When it seemed God was calling her to write about angels, she did. Third, persist. Even when there seemed to be no market for a book about angels, Joan persisted. Fourth, find creative solutions. When bookstores would not carry the first book from a new publisher, Joan found creative ways to publicize the book and get stores to carry it. With so many problems, a grumpy old grouch would have quit and spent the time complaining. Joan did what was needed and became a best-selling author.

Sweet old ladies do not all become best-selling authors. But everyone who does what is necessary, follows God's call, persists in the face of difficulties, and finds creative solutions will end up as a successful person. Success is not measured by fame or fortune. Success is being that woman who has found what needs to be done and has persisted in doing it.

NINE

Know When to Quit

A sweet old lady knows when to quit. A grumpy old grouch must be forced out.

Our church had a wonderful choir. The most faithful member of the choir was Cathy Camp. In fact, Cathy had been the most faithful member of the choir for over fifty years. Through good times and bad, Cathy had always been in the choir loft, lifting her strong voice in song. People would say that years ago Cathy had a good voice and was an asset to the choir. Everyone respected Cathy and no one wanted to hurt her feelings, so all anyone would say were things like, "She certainly is faithful," and "I wish you could have heard her sing years ago." What was left unsaid was that it often took Cathy some time to land on the right note. Cathy would still sing enthusiastically with her strong voice, making it impossible to hide that she was sometimes off pitch.

I'll always remember Aunt Cathy and how wonderful people were to her in her declining years. As a teen, I promised myself I would learn a lesson from Cathy Camp and know when to quit. That's not always easy to do. As an adult, I've learned to appreciate that many senior citizens make a positive contribution to a choir. The secret is knowing when to quit. We see the issue most clearly in others when they are past their prime. But knowing when to quit is not just a problem for those who are aging. It happens to all of us in different stages of life.

In grade school our daughter Sharon made a wise choice in friends. One of Sharon's friends, Barbara, was a fun person of good character. She was not only bright but was also gifted in many ways. She was an especially good oboe player and also excelled in sports, drama, and church leadership. Although a member of another church, she often attended our church's youth activities with our daughter, and my husband was like a second pastor to her. I'll never forget the late-night telephone call she made to my husband from the University of Miami where she was completing her Ph.D. studies in marine biology. Taking stock of herself, she realized she received her greatest fulfillment in life when she was taking part in some kind of Christian service. Barbara felt she was being called to Christian ministry. After graduating from Princeton Theological Seminary, she was on the pastoral staff of a church in Oklahoma. Today she has a promising career in the chaplain's corps of the U.S. Army.

We met again recently at our daughter's home in New Jersey for our grandson Jonathan's dedication. "Are you still playing the oboe?" I asked.

"No," she answered. "Playing the oboe is something that takes continuous practice. I have learned I can't do everything I am interested in if I am going to do some things well. I have to make choices, so I donated my oboe to a school that needed an instrument." A wise choice! She enjoyed her oboe and she could still play the instrument well, but she gave it up to focus on other areas of life.

Sherwood Wirt, for many years the editor of *Decision* magazine, spoke recently at our local writer's conference. "Perhaps the most important advice I can give you is this," he admonished the aspiring new authors in the group. "If you want to be a writer, you cannot do everything else. Writing takes time and effort. You cannot add it to a schedule that is already too full." Anything valuable is worth sacrificing for something else of value.

Know When to Quit

Persistence is a virtue, but it is not virtuous to be stubborn or obstinate. At times we need to examine our activities and habits and ask the following questions:

1. Do I have the time to keep doing this?

My neighbor Tonya in Seattle was a delightful woman who was willing to help wherever needed. Because she was capable and conscientious, she was often asked to serve on committees and boards. Each year she took on more responsibilities without giving up any of her previous jobs. The last time I asked, she told me she belonged to fifteen different organizations and held at least one position or office in each of them. "They are all good organizations doing good things," she told me. The people in her church, clubs, and civic groups all admired Tonya, but increasingly they were becoming frustrated with her because she was so overcommitted. In time, the strain of trying to do so much affected Tonya in several ways. Her personality, naturally sparkling and joyful, increasingly became more irritable and defensive as the work piled up, and people began to criticize when she didn't have things done on time. As the stress increased, Tonya found it harder to sleep at night, and she had more sick days. Everyone who knew Tonya agreed: She was trying to do more than she could, but they would repeat the old cliché, "When you need to get something done, ask a busy woman." She needed to stop some of her activities, and Tonya herself would say, "I know I'm overloaded, but . . ."

A wise woman once told me, "I cannot do everything. I cannot even do all the good things I would like to do. I do no one a favor if I attempt to do more than I can handle. Before I accept any new task, I must ask myself, 'What am I now doing that I can stop doing?'"

2. Is this the priority it once was?

Joining the Newcomers' Club when you were new in town may have been important as a way to make new friends and learn about the community. A year later, when you have made friends and found a church home, it may no longer be important. This year's priority may be to accept a leadership position in your church group.

3. Would it be more profitable for me to do something else?

The motivational experts often talk about the person who is too busy working to get ahead in life. The business in their daily routine keeps them from discovering new opportunities that may be far more beneficial for them. Many conscientious people fill all their hours working diligently on the tasks they have been doing for years. They never stop to ask if there are new opportunities or better ways for their skills to be used. "I don't have time to even think about doing anything else," they say.

Churches and volunteer organizations take advantage of this kind of mind-set. If you will allow them, they will take advantage of your willingness to serve by giving you the jobs no one else wants to do. Once you accept, they will expect you to continue year after year. When no one else would take the position, Marci agreed to serve as secretary of her garden club. She discovered that she was the kind of person who could focus on only one thing at a time. If she were taking notes so she could accurately write the minutes, she found she could not join in the discussion. She had limited secretarial skills, and it took her forever to type out the minutes of the meeting, but she was faithful. Marci always turned in well-written minutes and they were always on time. She promptly took care of the club's correspondence even though it took a great amount of time. Soon her church group and another club pressured Marci to become their secretary "because she was so good at the job." Marci was frustrated because she was spending so much time doing secretarial work. It kept her from the opportunity to use her true gift of creative leadership.

Helen does not spend hours taking minutes, but she is frustrated because she is kept busy baking nut bread and cookies, things she can do well. But her baking leaves her little time to do the things she really loves.

4. Do I have the ability to do this well? Is this the best use of my time?

Joan Wester Anderson, the best-selling author of *Where Angels Walk* and other books, was working in the church kitchen when her pastor walked in. "What are you doing here?" he asked.

"I'm helping with the Boy Scout pancake breakfast," Joan replied. She was a little surprised by his question. The church hall was filled with people eating pancakes, and the pastor had been chatting with the families. He knew this was a pancake breakfast and that Joan's son was in the Boy Scout troop.

"But why are you here?" her pastor persisted.

"Well, they needed help," Joan replied. "And Pastor, I love the Lord and want to do my part. I haven't done much that was sacrificial this month, so here I am working in the kitchen."

There was a twinkle in the pastor's eye and tenderness in his voice. "Joan, everyone knows that you hate cooking and working in the kitchen. Besides, you're not very good at it. You are good at writing. If you would have spent time writing publicity, we would have had a far greater turnout, and it would have helped the troop much more."

"But, Pastor, writing the publicity would have been so easy for me. I could have done it in just a few minutes. That really wouldn't have been a sacrifice for me," the professional author replied.

"The Lord doesn't delight in making us miserable," the pastor replied. "He wants us to do the things we are good at and enjoy. When we use the gifts he has given us, we can serve the Lord with gladness, and everyone benefits."

Joan has not worked in the church kitchen since that conversation. She does tithe her time, only now she often uses her writing ability to help her church and other groups and individuals. She is serving the Lord with gladness.

If you find yourself stuck, spending much of your time doing things you dislike, it may be that what you are doing is not what you should be doing. Take the initiative to make a change.

5. Has the time come for someone else to do this?

Keep life fresh! Avoid settling into ruts, especially ones that make life humdrum. Yes, some activities you should continue year after year. If you enjoy doing them and you are making a contribution, keep on keeping on. If it is a vital part of life, like exercise and a daily quiet time, persist even through dry spells. If it is a worthwhile tradition, continue it and cherish the memories.

Even with treasured traditions, we need to ask if the time has come for someone else to take up the mantle. For example, do grown children have to wait until Grandmother and Grandfather die before they can begin to cook and carve the Thanksgiving turkey? As our children grow older, we need to make transitions. All too often we treat our children as children, even when they are adults. This robs us from nurturing, healthy relationships.

In our wider contacts, we need to be open to giving new people an opportunity for significant involvement. My husband and I shared in the thrilling experience of pastoring a growing, dynamic church in Park Forest, Illinois. The town was known as "the organization man's suburb" because almost everyone worked for one of the large corporations. These were bright, capable people. Ninety-five percent of all the adults in Park Forest had a college education. They were the junior executives, on their way up. At that time the rule was that every advancement meant a transfer, so the average time a family spent in Park Forest was three to four years. It was a challenge to reach these young families quickly. Most of these young couples had no experience in church leadership. Their mothers and fathers had been the leaders in the churches where they grew up. It was exciting to recruit them to be teachers, committee and board members, workers, and leaders. They became excited, too. For most of them this was the first time they had really been involved for more than just attending services. They grew, they blossomed, they were blessed, and they blessed others in return.

When the promotion came, we rejoiced with them and sent them off with our prayers and best wishes. They moved to a new city where their corporation had another branch. They threw themselves into their new job assignment. Eagerly they went to a new church and volunteered. Then they would call and write us, often heartbroken. One woman wrote, "We had found such joy in working in the church in Park Forest that we volunteered to help in our new church wherever needed. When time passed and we were not asked to do anything, we volunteered again . . . and again. Finally we were told that every position in the church was being held by someone who had been serving for many years. However if we really wanted to do something, we could polish the piano in the church parlor!"

If new people are to become a part of an organization, they need to be able to take part in a meaningful way that uses their talents. This is a good reason to stop and let someone else begin to serve.

Charlotte had been the chair of the flower committee in her church for many years. "I'd like to be free of this responsibility," she confided in me. "I've done it for so long; it only seems fair that someone else should take over, but everyone says I've done such a good job that no one would dare to follow me. The nominating committee can't find anyone to take my place. What should I do?"

"Resign," I told her. "They will never find anyone to take your place as long as you continue." How often I have found that to be true. Sometimes when a person like Charlotte has held a position for a long time and has been outstanding, others are hesitant to be compared with her. Often people think Charlotte does not really want to be replaced—after all, she has been doing this for years, hasn't she? Only after there is a vacancy will people know that Charlotte's feelings will not be hurt when someone else takes over.

Bea ran the boutique at the retirement home. The proceeds went to the resident council to fund special activities. Those living in the retirement home loved having greeting cards, small gifts, and personal necessities available. In every way it was a success. Bea continued to run the boutique even when her eyesight began to fail, but she realized the time was coming when she would no longer be able to manage. She tried to find a replacement. Several residents did take over for a short while, but each resigned after a few weeks. The reason? Bea never let go. Even when someone new had the responsibility, Bea would tell them how to run things. Capable people, who would have done an excellent job with the boutique, soon realized that Bea would never give up control. The lesson? When it's time to quit, quit! Be willing to give help and encouragement to your successor, but let her work in her own way.

Choose what you do wisely. Do your work faithfully and well. Remember, no one is indispensable. Know when to quit.

TEN

Take Time to Smell the Roses

A sweet old lady takes time to enjoy life. A grumpy old grouch is too busy complaining.

ost people are just too busy. Few women would argue with this point, but they never stop to realize that in almost every case we can do something about it! Eugenia Price in her book, *A Woman's Choice*, writes, "One thing sure, no woman is her balanced best, no woman can think clearly and make wise decisions when she's physically and nervously exhausted. And still, woman after woman chastises herself and wonders why her temper doesn't vanish like an April snowflake, when she only needs to slow down! Woman after woman blames her husband or her children when their communication breaks down, and all the time she is perhaps just too exhausted to communicate."

So often our difficulty is that we try to pack more into a day than we are capable of doing. This is especially true as we get more experience in life. (What I really mean is, I can't do as much now as when I was younger, but I hate to admit it, so I cram my schedule as full as I did twenty years ago.) If we are trying to tackle too much, we will always be frustrated.

The Problem

Why do we take on too much? Let's be honest. Often it has more to do with a woman's ego than anything else. If you are competent, it's very enticing to say yes, especially when there are those who will tell you how capable you are and heap praises on your pretty head every time you perform.

Most of us feel like helpless victims where our work and activity schedules are concerned. We feel as though we have no control over many of the things expected of us. I confess this has been entirely true of me. Over lunch with one of my favorite people, Joan Wester Anderson, I shared my hectic schedule. At that time it included a deadline for a book, a full schedule of speaking engagements, twenty angel teas to be served in my home in the next few weeks, as well as running my angel shop and catalog business. Joan looked at me wisely and said, "Marilynn, I know what it's like because I have been there myself. I'm speaking from experience when I say you can't keep it up. You have to take back control of your life."

"How did you do it?" I asked.

"I learned to say no," she replied. "My husband made me stand in front of a mirror and practice saying no."

"Really?" I asked incredulously. "You really practiced saying no?"

"Yes," Joan laughed. "It's not as easy as you think. That's why you are in trouble. It's hard to say no. Let me guess. When you do say no, don't you give a reason?"

"Well, yes," I agreed. "Isn't that the best thing to do?"

"Not at all," Joan answered. "Whatever reason you give only opens the door for them to negotiate a yes answer. Let's try it. Suppose I call and ask to schedule a Christmas tea in your home. What would you say?"

"That's easy," I responded. "I would tell you that all the weekends are taken from now until Christmas."

Joan had a twinkle in her eye as she said, "You've just admitted you don't have every weekday committed. I would push for a Tuesday, Wednesday, or Thursday, and you would probably schedule me, wouldn't you?"

"Yes," I admitted.

"There's the problem. You know you have too much to do, but you don't firmly close the door to adding one more event."

"What should I say?" I asked.

"I'm sorry. I'm completely booked for Christmas teas this year. We could choose a date for next year. My first opening is in February. Would you like to set a date for a Valentine tea?" Joan continued, "With an answer like this you have said a firm no. You keep control of your life. You set the alternative that you can live with. But because this does not come naturally for you, you have to practice."

I have been practicing, and I've gotten pretty good at it. Learning to order one's life is a slow process for most of us.

The First Step

The way to begin is by eliminating everything that is possible to eliminate. Your family will probably cheer you on, but your friends and club members may not understand. Your fellow church members will probably be the least accepting. The best approach is to admit to them that you feel guilty about being too busy. Nine times out of ten, they do, too. You will probably be surprised at the support you get if you ask their understanding and cooperation. Of course, some may not understand. Some workaholics are convinced that everyone needs to be as busy as they are. The overachievers and perfectionists often think others should be as active as they are. Then, too, other women may have different priorities than you. The activity or group that is most important to them may be the least significant to you. If they try to make you feel guilty, don't fall for it. God doesn't want you to be harried and overworked. Don't let someone who likes to play God trap you into feeling a false guilt. Ask yourself, "What difference will it make fifty years from now if I don't . . ."

So much of what we do, we do so that people will like us. "The girls will never forgive you if you don't accept the presidency again!" Oh, yes, they will. And if they don't, it's a false guilt they are trying to heap on you. Don't fall for it. If you should say no, God will be pleased when you *do* say no, and you have nothing to feel guilty about.

A Lesson from History

The story is old, so old that it may date back to biblical times. A recent convert, filled with zeal for his newfound faith, was dismayed to see the apostle John playing with two pet birds. "There is so much important work to be done," the young convert admonished. "How can you waste your time in play?"

John was not defensive. He simply smiled and replied, "The bow that is always bent soon ceases to shoot straight!"

The aged apostle could remember the time years ago when he and the disciples were with Jesus. John had been working night and day. There were so many people with needs and so much ministry to be done. Then Jesus called the Twelve aside and said, "Come apart and rest a while." They left the place of busy service to go to a quiet place. Jesus understood the importance of balancing work with rest—serving others and replenishing one's own soul. One wise commentator observed that if we don't take time to come apart we will likely fall apart.

Often we are slow to learn this lesson. When my husband, Bill, led a men's retreat, he began by asking the men to introduce themselves by giving their names and what they did with their leisure time. Each of the men gave a variation of the same theme: "I don't have any leisure time, but if I did, this is what I would like to do." When they had finished, Bill pointed out that if in fact they had no leisure time, if all they did was work at their business and at home, then their lives were out of balance. In the discussion that followed, the men not only agreed that they did work too much but that they felt guilty if they took time out to smell the roses.

We Learn as Children

This is true of many of us women as well. From the time we were children, the importance of doing our work was stressed. You can remember being congratulated when you worked hard. Do you ever remember receiving praise for not working? Yes, probably if you enjoyed reading a book in your spare time, you were praised. But wasn't that because your parents saw reading as "doing something constructive" that would help you in your schoolwork?

Children are rightly taught to accept responsibility, to study and to learn at home and at school, to make their beds, and help with the housework. Children are taught to feel good when work is completed and done well. Unfortunately, few parents teach their children how to relax or how to have fun. (The exception is that we do teach our children the skills of competitive sports.) How fortunate is the child whose parents celebrate a lazy summer day without adding, "But we really should have been working."

Psychologists have now discovered that daydreaming is important in a child's development and plays a key role in the development of creativity that helps a person adjust to life. Daydreaming is not just for when all the important things are done. Taking time to daydream is one of the important tasks of life.

Enjoy Yourself!

To become well-rounded, mature adults, we need to recapture a childlike sense of wonder, the ability to delight in the color of an egg yolk in a blue bowl, the feel of the breeze on our face, and the smell of cookies that come from the oven.

So be responsible. Work hard and accomplish a lot. But take time to smell the roses and don't feel guilty when you do. Enjoy yourself! Enjoy the people around you. Enjoy God. That's not being selfish. Theologians tell us that is what God created us for. Let's face it—if you are not enjoying life, other people are not going to enjoy being around you. You are on your way to becoming that grumpy old grouch instead of a sweet old lady. If you are not taking time now to enjoy life, you will not know how to do it when you are old. Unless you take care of yourself, you are going to be limited in how much you will be able to help others.

Yes, satisfaction is to be found in work well-done and accomplishments that are a part of our occupation. This year I have really enjoyed being the author of the book, *A Rustle of Angels*. I found it rewarding when the book sold over 300,000 copies. It was thrilling to accept the print media award from the Excellence in Media Foundation at Sardi's in New York City. It was exciting to be on countless radio and television talk shows. It has been a delight to speak in churches of all sizes and denominations. My husband tells people I speak from cathedrals to casinos. That is literally true. This fall I was on the program of the International Women's Conference at the Crystal Cathedral, and a few weeks later I spoke at the MGM Grand Hotel in Las Vegas. I got a feeling of joy and satisfaction in all this. This is my occupation. I work hard at what I do, and I find it rewarding.

Yet, I still need a plan to help me take time to smell the roses. I have found a majority of women share this need. Most of us have learned to plan our work. Too many of us have never learned the importance of planning that part of our lives that is not work-related. Take time to plan to smell the roses.

Life's Little Pleasures

Make your daily life enjoyable. Taking a bath or shower is a necessity. Why not plan to make it a delightful luxury? It costs only a few cents to add a favorite bath oil. It takes only two or three minutes more to luxuriate in the experience of bathing. Change your attitude. Bathing need not be a compulsory chore. With a minimum of planning, it can be a time of personal pampering.

You Deserve a Break Today

The law requires that employers must give employees who work an eight-hour shift not only time for lunch but also a ten-minute break in the morning and afternoon. The intent of the law is to safeguard the health and well-being of the workers. Studies have shown that employees who take breaks get more work done during the day than those who work straight through. Of course, the person who uses her break as a time to cram in as much personal business as possible defeats the entire purpose. They are the losers. Homemakers and women who are self-employed often do not realize the importance of taking breaks. When we have the freedom to set our own schedules, we should be at least as kind to ourselves as the law requires employers to be to their employees.

Add Loveliness to Your Life

If you are like me, it doesn't work to stop in the middle of the afternoon and collapse into a comfortable chair. It makes me feel sleepy, and when break time is over, I find it hard to get up and get going. What works best for me is to plan a time in my afternoon activities where I set aside my work and clear my mind for a few minutes. Instead of doing nothing, I choose to do something that is relaxing and a change of pace. When I lived in England, I discovered how delightful and refreshing afternoon tea could be. My friend, the author Emilie Barnes, agrees. She writes in her best-selling book, *If Teacups Could Talk*, that the potential stress reduction of teatime is enormous.

"Tea takes time—and that's part of the magic. You can't hurry it without losing something vital. The act of making and drinking tea forces us to slow down—and I truly believe our bodies and spirits are desperate to slow down from the frantic pace our culture sets for us today. People in our society don't like to wait, but you simply cannot hurry a good pot of tea."

First, you must wait until the water is boiling. I like to use my electric tea kettle. If I'm just making tea for myself, it doesn't take long for one cup of water to boil. When my husband joins me or when friends drop by for tea, it takes a little longer for the pot to boil. While I'm waiting, I set out the teacups and arrange a plate of cookies. Next, tea takes time to steep. That's a lovely three to five minutes, no longer, or the tea gets bitter. If I'm alone, I carry the tray to my favorite chair and wait in peace, using the time to think or pray or just relax until the tea reaches its fragrant amber. If I'm with friends, this is a wonderful time to talk.

Emilie Barnes writes, "No, none of these things is absolutely necessary. You can always go back to microwaving water and fishing your cookie directly from the package. You can drink your tea, standing up at the counter, or gulp it as you run out the door. But again, you'll be missing the opportunity. You see, boiling water in a kettle is part of the ritual. Arranging the tea tray is part of a ritual. Preparing and enjoying tea is a ritual in itself. I love what my friend Yoli Brogger calls it: 'a ceremony of loveliness.' And I believe with all my heart that human beings crave ritual and ceremony (and loveliness) in our lives."

It's Your Choice

Perhaps tea isn't your thing. Something else may be. You know what it is that brings you enjoyment and relaxation and can be done as a welcome break in your daily routine. Alice works a crossword puzzle. She finds it fun and considers it educational as well. The concentration needed turns her thoughts away from her work but places no stress on her. A puzzle can fill any block of time she chooses to spend.

Helen is a homemaker. Each morning at ten she plays the piano for fifteen minutes. "I just play for my own amazement," she smiles. Ramona has a regular letter carrier who delivers her mail every day within a few minutes of two-thirty in the afternoon. Ramona eagerly looks forward to this time and has developed a routine to help her enjoy this mail break to the fullest. She sits at her rolltop desk. When she comes across a bill, it goes directly into the compartment for bills to be paid. She scans the junk mail as she comes across it. She can tell in a few seconds that many fliers have no interest for her. These are quickly dropped into the wastebasket at her side. The magazines and catalogs that she would like to go through later are placed in a pile. She will read these at the end of the day as she unwinds before going to bed. This leaves her desk clear except for the personal letters. Since she is a faithful letter writer, she almost always receives a letter or two. "I like to save the personal mail for the end," Ramona says. "I feel good because I have taken care of the clutter of the junk mail and have been orderly about the bills and business items. Then reading the cards and letters from friends and family is like the dessert after a meal. It is my favorite time of the day."

Jane, on the other hand, delights in doing nothing. "I just lean back in my chair and unwind," she says. "What can be more relaxing than doing nothing?"

Her friend Mabel objects. "If I lean back in my chair, I go to sleep. If I fall asleep during the afternoon, it leaves me lethargic for the next hour or two, and I can't sleep at night."

"I can," Cathy says, almost proudly. "I can close my eyes and fall asleep almost any time, but I wake up refreshed in five minutes or less. I don't need much sleep at night—six hours at the most. A short afternoon nap never keeps me awake at night."

"I guess that proves each of us is different," Ruth replies. "I would never look forward to an afternoon nap of any kind, but I love to spend ten minutes on my treadmill. It keeps my body in shape and makes my mind alert for the next session at the computer."

"I don't have any space for a treadmill," Esther adds. "I work in an office downtown, and except when it rains, I take a brisk walk."

"I use my break time to keep spiritually fit," Rowena shares. "I carry a small devotional book in my purse and look forward to this extra quiet time in the day."

As I listened to my friends talk, I was aware how different they are. Each has her own way to relax, a different activity (or lack of it) that she enjoys. What is important is that they know how to enjoy a break, they plan for it, and they do it. They take the time to smell the roses, and they are better because of it.

Evenings Are Important

When our children were young and at home, they would often repeat, "Mondays are fun days." That was our family night. We considered it to be the most important commitment on our calendar and took time planning how we would spend it together.

My husband and I also plan a date night each week. It need not be expensive. In the early days of our marriage when money was tight, it was sometimes "dinner" at McDonald's, where we lingered over a cup of coffee to chat and share our problems and dreams. We had to plan ahead for this when our children were young. After they left the nest, we had more freedom. We did not need to arrange for sitters or take the children's schedules into consideration. This very freedom led to our date night's becoming irregular and haphazard. Finally we realized what was happening and returned to setting a specific day. We believe having a date night is important, even for couples who have retired. It sets aside a time that is recognized as being special for a relationship. It helps a couple plan to do things together that might never be done otherwise.

In addition to couples pausing in their routine to relax, everyone needs to stop to reflect, recreate, and refresh. Every evening should include some time to smell the roses. Our married daughter, Sharon, believes in using the swing on their front porch. You have to learn to relax, clear your mind of all work and worries, and just rock. Talking with a friend or spouse can also enrich the experience, as long as the relaxation rules are kept. "Some day I'll write a book about the art," she chuckles. "I'll call it *Rocking on the Front Porch of Your Life*."

One single woman, a professional speaker, schedules one night each week for her "reading night." She considers that to be as important an appointment as her speaking engagements. Another friend has a music night. She plays her favorite recordings and takes time to listen and enjoy the music.

Let's not waste precious downtime. Television can be a terrible time-waster. Evenings can be lost watching whatever is on the boob tube, even though it is not particularly enjoyable. Too much TV, like too much of anything, takes away the pleasure and enjoyment. But television can also be a great joy and delight. It is not true that there is nothing good on television. Some nights nothing is worth watching, but on other nights some programs are outstanding. It is worth the effort to discover what is good and then to watch actively, giving the program your full attention.

Take Time Away

Take a few moments to smell the roses. After you have planted, watered, fertilized, and pruned the bushes, it is even more rewarding to pick the roses and arrange them in a beautiful bouquet that will brighten your home for days. It's wonderful to take a few minutes a day for a spot of loveliness. Plan a different kind of reward for yourself, such as an entire special day or a vacation.

Anyone can and everyone should take time away. This chapter is being written during the week that Cal Ripken broke Lou Gehrig's fifty-six-year-old record for playing in 2,130 consecutive baseball games. He has not missed a game for thirteen years because of sickness or injury. It is a remarkable feat. But Cal has had time off. Baseball games are not scheduled every day, and he has vacation time during the off-season.

Our daily newspaper, the *Riverside-Press Enterprise*, reported that a local worker, Jorge Vasquez, has not missed a day of work in twenty-four years, not even for sickness. "Ripken is a hero to the working class. Vasquez, and others like him, are heroes *in* the working class," the paper reported. Vasquez is a supervisor at Fleetwood Enterprises, an RV manufacturer. Amazingly, he has taken only two days of vacation in twenty-four years. Year after year when his vacation comes up, Vasquez simply takes a pass on the month he is allowed, choosing instead to work, even though he won't get paid for the lost vacation. "I like my job," he says simply.

How wonderful to be able to go twenty-four years without having to call in sick once! The national average is to take four sick days a year or a total of ninety-six in a twenty-four-year period. Jorge Vasquez must be blessed with exceptionally good health. We commend him for his faithfulness in attendance and willingness to work. Listen to Vasquez: "When I came from Mexico, I made up my mind to work and work," he said. "It is what I can do to buy a house and things I like for my family." There's his motivation—to provide for his family. Great!

When reading the newspaper account, I applauded this diligent worker. Still, some nagging questions came to my mind. He has worked hard to help his family. Wouldn't he have helped his family more by spending his vacation with them instead of going to work? What did it say to his family when they saw that he chose to spend his vacation working without pay? Weren't there places he would like to go? Things he would like to do? Memories he would like to make with his family? Things he wanted to learn? Ways he could help others? If he had taken some time to smell the roses, wouldn't he have been refreshed and able to do his job better?

A vacation breaks our normal routine. I find many blessings in our vacation times; however, getting ready to leave has always been a hassle for me. It meant getting work finished and tying up loose ends so I would be able to leave. It took a few years for me to see this as a benefit in itself. When I was a schoolteacher, the last few weeks of the term were always busy. When the grades were all recorded, the last book checked in, and the final reports made, I had a feeling of closure. What a sense of relief! Preparations for a vacation serve a similar function. Although we may be pushed to meet the deadlines of work to be completed before we take off, there are values in pulling loose ends together and finishing tasks that need to be done.

One of the keys to happiness is having something to look forward to. Planning and anticipating a time away is a joy in itself. The change in schedule and freedom from the daily routine that a vacation brings is therapeutic. Vacation experiences create memories that are cherished for a lifetime.

We must resist the temptation to postpone vacations. There are always reasons that seem compelling. Beware of this one, especially: *I am too busy to take a vacation right now.* If you are too busy, then you really need to take time off. There may never come a time when you will not be busy.

I was talking to a hospital group on this subject. Interrupting my speech, a woman walked to the podium and handed me a note. Everyone sat with baited breath. Was there an emergency and someone was being called out? I took the paper and read the message out loud. It said, "If you don't take time to smell the roses, you may soon be pushing up the daisies." There was a startled silence, then the room broke into applause. The point had been made!

It's good to take time to smell the roses away from home. It can be more important than you think.

Come to the Party!

One of the greatest stories ever told can be understood on several levels. A man had two sons, as different as night and day. The younger son pushed to receive his inheritance while he could still enjoy it. He took the money, went to a far country, and squandered it on riotous living. When he had spent everything, he hit bottom and returned home. His waiting father, overjoyed at his son's return, threw the party of the century. But the older son refused to come. He kept working in the fields. He made it clear that he always worked and never wasted his time playing or going to parties. The father went to entreat the older son to come and join the party, but he would not.

One of the points this parable makes is that the prodigal was wrong because he refused to accept responsibility and work. But his older brother was wrong also because he was a drudge, always working, not enjoying life.

Commenting on this parable, Bruce Larson has written that there are three types of people in the world. The first face life with the attitude, *There is no party*. They view life as a daily grind. The second group feel, *There is a party, but I'm not invited*. They do not believe they are entitled to find joy. The third group eagerly face the day, thinking, *There is a party, and I'm invited*. Larson writes that Jesus saw salvation as being more than release from guilt and forgiveness from sin. It was also entering into a vibrant, joyful lifestyle. "I have come that they may have life," Jesus said, "and have it to the full" (John 10:10). Larson writes that in the story of the Prodigal Son, Jesus is giving the invitation to salvation by saying, "Come to the party."

Yesterday I visited my friend, Vicki Kvenvick, who was home recovering from stomach surgery. When she asked what I was writing, I told her about this chapter. She shared with me a poem, taken from an old greeting card that she had framed on the wall. This anonymous poet said it well:

> Let me take time to see the flowers
> That grow by the side of the road.
> Let me take time to lend a hand
> That will lighten another's load.
>
> Let me take time to hear the sounds
> Of happy children at play.
> Let me take time to visit a friend
> Who might be lonely today.
>
> Let me take time to share my thoughts
> With those who are dear to me,
> And let me take time for a quiet hour
> To spend, Lord, alone with thee.

ELEVEN

Make New Friends

A sweet old lady makes new friends. A grumpy
old grouch complains all her friends are gone.

They came for an angel tea at my house. It was to celebrate Sonia's eightieth birthday. It was a gift from Ann,
Sonia's daughter-in-law, who had made the arrangements and
who had invited all of Sonia's friends—all four of Sonia's
friends. The four were the beauticians at the shop where Sonia
had her hair done each week. Ann explained that as Sonia's
husband had grown older, he had retreated more into himself.
He wanted Sonia to be at home with him all the time. The
only exception was Sunday morning when he grudgingly
agreed to let her go to the beauty parlor before she attended
church. The only people Sonia had any regular contact with
outside her house were the four beauty operators she saw
once a week. Sonia wisely had made the effort to get to know
them and to make friends not only of her regular beautician
but also of the other three girls in the shop. No matter that
they were young enough to be her daughters and one was
young enough to be her granddaughter. Sonia was determined to make friends, and she did the best she could in her
difficult situation. This outing was the first Sonia had had for
a long time, and we made the most of it. When she left, she
gave me a hug and said, "Thank you. This has been the most
beautiful day of my life."

Isolates. That's the word sociologists use to describe individuals who withdraw from society. Greta Garbo was not the only one to say, "I want to be alone." About thirty percent of Americans over sixty-five live in isolation. They do leave their homes to go to the store or to the doctor's office, but they only venture out when it is necessary. If asked, they say they have no friends. A typical response is, "All my friends have died."

It can happen to anyone. It is likely to happen to you unless you choose to make new friends. It's not only that our old friends die. In our modern society people move away or their life situation changes.

This happens not only in our golden years; it happens all through life. Alice was my best friend as I went through high school and college. We thought we would always get together and talk late into the night, but Alice and her husband became missionaries and moved to Japan. Like most couples today, my husband and I have moved several times, and we are thousands of miles away from the town where we grew up. We have had to go through the process of making new friends over and over.

If a woman does not learn the skills of making friends and make the effort to have new friends when she's young and in midlife, she will find it harder to do when she is older. The earlier we choose a lifestyle where making friends is important to us, the easier it will be to make and keep friendships to the end of our lives. The reason some old people feel so lonely is that they were already lonely without knowing it before they retired. In this, as in many other aspects of life, growing older reveals what a woman really is, although she may not wish to see it.

For the lonely, yes, even for the isolates, there is good news: Everyone can change. Making friends is more difficult for some, especially if it means changing lifelong patterns, but it can be done and it is worth the effort. There is truth for women of all ages in the little round we sang as girls around the campfire:

Make new friends, but keep the old.
One is silver, but the other gold.

Begin at Home

Dr. V. Raymond Edman was the president of Wheaton College in my student days. He was held in high regard by the academic community, and the students not only respected him but had a genuine affection for him. Years later as we reminisce, we remember that when he referred to Mrs. Edman he always called her "friend wife." Everyone knew this described their relationship well. What a beautiful example it was to the student body.

When a person grows older, it is natural to develop a deeper intimacy with a mate. If a couple has been happy together in their earlier years, growing old together can be a time of real blessing. Of course, no married couple is able to grow and come to maturity without encountering conflicts. In a healthy relationship the difficult periods lead to frank dialogue. At times this results in compromise. Other times this leads the husband and wife to gradually accept the other as he or she is. As new problems arise, the dialogue is less tense, while at the same time it is even more fruitful.

The wise couple place the conflicts they face in this broader context. They place a priority on their relationship and know that the way they approach problem solving affects not only the present issue but also the climate of their life together for years to come.

Many couples do not grow together. Sometimes two individuals stand in opposition to each other and battle constantly. At other times one partner, to safeguard the peace and apparent unity, capitulates to the tyranny of the other. He or she may avoid any subject that gives rise to conflict. Unfortunately this also hides a portion of that person's life, and a trench is gradually dug between them. Even though they are still married to each other, they become more like a bachelor and a spinster.

Two people may learn to live like this without much pain when they are in their active years because each has his or her own interests and activities. When retirement comes, one or both no longer have the interests of their occupation or contacts with their fellow workers. There are fewer opportunities for socialization. The children are no longer at home. They find themselves alone together, face-to-face, and they have nothing to say to each other. Instead of happiness, they are increasingly bored with each other.

The wise woman builds a strong marriage through the years. If this has not been done before the retirement years, she will do all she can to change the patterns and develop a friendship with her husband for the remaining years.

Make New Friends

Dr. Paul Tournier, in his excellent book, *Learn to Grow Old*, writes, "Sometimes one hears it said that it is not easy to form new friendships once one is no longer young. . . . My closest friends from the period of my childhood and youth are nearly all dead and gone. My wife, too, has lost many of hers. But we have lots of new friendships, wonderful friendships with men and women who are mostly younger than we and who certainly play their part in keeping us young in heart and mind. Some of our closest friends we have known for only a few years."

The nice thing about friends your own age is that you have much in common. If you both have small children, this gives you a lot to talk about. If you have teenagers in common, you have many opportunities to give each other support and share in the joys and trials of parenting. If you have come to the retirement years, you have a lifetime of experiences and a maturity that only years can give to enrich your relationships. Common ground can establish a basis to friendship when both people find issues in common, whether their concerns are diapers or Medicare.

As Dr. Tournier has testified, there can be wonderful friendships between people of different ages. Patrice Verhines is such a friend for me. We met because we were both active in church affairs. I enjoy being with Patrice; she enjoys my company. Besides our age, we are different in many ways.

Patrice loves to sew, while needlework has always been at the bottom of my list of enjoyable hobbies. Her husband, Bob, is an expert carpenter by trade. My husband remembers the difficulty he had in making a passing grade in wood shop in the eighth grade. My Bill would rather read and study or write books. Put us together, especially when Bob and Patrice's children are there, and you would think we are family. The difference in age adds to our relationship. The ways we are dissimilar enrich our closeness. Bob was able to repair my mother's chair that meant so much to me, while my husband baptized their children. It makes sense, doesn't it, to have friends of different ages? Young mothers sometimes like to have conversations besides diaper talk, and seniors tire of talking about life's increasing aches and pains.

But How to Make Friends?

Friendship has endured and persisted throughout history. Some cultures recognize the importance of friends so much that they are structured into their society. For example, the Didinga of West Africa have an enforced "best friend" system. In the United States the making of friends is left to each individual.

Almost every American would agree that having friends is good. In part that explains the success of Dale Carnegie's book, *How to Win Friends and Influence People.* The book has gone through ninety-five printings and has sold over seven million copies. Written in 1936, it is still being sold in bookstores everywhere. This says three things about our society. First, people want to make friends. Second, we think we can discover the way to win friends by reading a book. Third, we find it hard to manage the friendships we do have.

We must be truthful: No person can go from being friendless to having friends by reading a book. That is true of Dale Carnegie's book and especially true of this book you are currently reading. You can learn to pass the written examination for a driver's license by studying a book, but the art of friendship is based on more than memorizing rules or procedures.

There are principles that are important in making and keeping friends. Even though some of these seem so obvious, many people ignore these and wonder why they do not have more friends. Here are a few practical ideas that help in making friends. This is not a complete list, but I would almost be willing to guarantee that if anyone with a positive attitude were to follow these suggestions she would find friends.

Go Where Friends Are to Be Found

A young woman wrote to the advice column of the newspaper. She wanted to marry a lawyer, she said, but didn't know how to find one. The columnist counseled her to spend time in the law library. Of course! To meet a lawyer, you go where the lawyers are.

To make friends, we must go where people are who can be our friend. We are limited in our choice of friendships by the boundaries we live in. If we stay at home and never go out, our choice of friends will be limited to the few people who come to our door. It is not realistic to expect to develop a full and meaningful relationship with the mail carrier! The elderly lady whose story is found at the beginning of this chapter went only to the beauty parlor and to church. But she got to church just a few minutes before the worship service began, and her husband was waiting for her immediately after the benediction. Her one chance for a conversation beyond "good morning" was at the beauty parlor. Fortunately she made the most of her limited contact.

Church can be a wonderful place to meet people, but if a woman wants to make friends, she should attend the fellowship activities where there is the opportunity to mix and mingle and join a smaller group such as the women's ministry.

The rule is, Go where the people are. Go early and stay late so you will have time for conversation. If you are new in town, find the newcomers' club. If you are a mother with children, join the PTA. If you are a professional woman, attend your professional organization. If you enjoy gardening, try the garden club. If you are a senior, attend the AARP meetings, the activities at the senior center, and/or join your church's senior adult Sunday school class. Widen your circle. Go where the people are and take the time to socialize. Someone may be waiting there to become you new friend.

Do What You Love

Common activities help draw people closer. Just don't attend meetings. Do something. Does the club serve refreshments? Volunteer to help serve and clean up. Does the group have a service project? Join in and work side by side with others. Take a course. Community colleges offer classes on almost everything. They can be a good place to meet people with common interests. Remember, go early and don't be in a hurry to leave. Talk to others who share your interests. Better yet, find some way to work with someone. Offer to share a ride to and from class. Do you enjoy travel? Sign up to go with a group.

Some would argue that you are more likely to find acquaintances rather than friends. Don't underestimate the value of acquaintances. Remember that friendships begin with acquaintances.

Do Something for Someone

When our daughter, Sharon Linnea, was a student at New York University, she made a special friend who was seventy-three years older than she—and she met her on the street. One autumn day in 1976 a number-3 bus rumbled down New York's Fifth Avenue and stopped at Twelfth Street. An elderly passenger saw that she would not be able to make that last long step from the bus to the ground. A woman standing behind her saw the problem and in a strong, firm voice she said to the bus driver, "Young man, this is a kneeling bus. Would you be kind enough to let it kneel?" The bus driver, somewhat put out, lowered the bus, and the woman safely made her way off the bus to the curb. Sharon was fascinated with the older woman who had come to the assistance of her fellow passenger and had called out to the bus driver.

Sharon ran into her again when they were both shopping at a local deli. Sharon met her again a few days later, this time on the street. The older woman was struggling to carry a large package. Sharon offered to help. As they walked, Sharon discovered the woman's name was Laura and that her apartment was only two blocks away from the college dorm in Greenwich Village. Over the next few weeks the two kept running into each other, and a friendship began to form. They met for dinner at Shakespeare's, a local restaurant. Laura seemed interested in Sharon's plans to become a writer. Laura confided that because of her failing eyesight she was having trouble answering her mail. Sharon offered to help, and Laura invited her to her apartment.

It was a homey, one-room apartment. The walls were lined from top to bottom with books and boxes of letters. Laura had brought up the mail. She thumbed through it and handed Sharon a poetry magazine. "I can't read the type," Laura said. "Do I have anything in it?"

Sharon was startled. Was Laura a poet? Sure enough, her name was there. The title of the poem was "I let the trees know I was there." Laura sat at her small writing desk with a satisfied smile on her face and recited the entire poem from memory.

More discoveries were to follow shortly. As Sharon went to place the magazine on the shelf, she saw a copy of *King David* by the American writer Stephen Vincent Benét. Sharon picked up the gold embossed volume. It was a first edition, autographed by the author in 1923. "Where did you ever get this?" she asked her new friend.

"Why, Tibbie was my baby brother," she replied with her eyes dancing merrily. Laura's brother was Stephen Vincent Benét. Sixty years ago the Benéts were one of America's foremost literary families. Laura herself had more than twenty books to her name.

"Why didn't you tell me?" Sharon asked.

"My dear," she replied, "you must always give people room to surprise you. If you don't, they'll probably act like the boring people you expect them to be. You must give God room to surprise you, too."

As their friendship deepened, Laura surprised her young friend again and again. She told exciting first-person anecdotes about the leading literary figures of the past who had been frequent guests in her family home. She told wonderful stories about people and places from a time Sharon never knew. Our daughter learned more about the literary world from this ninety-two-year-old woman with her soft, braided hair and proper hats than from any of her professors at New York University.

It all started because Sharon did a good turn and helped an old lady carry her packages home. Do something to help someone. It can be the start of a glorious friendship.

A Friend with a Broom

Lucille Calvert was there when the moving van pulled up to our new home in Park Forest. She was dressed for work—housework, that is, and she was carrying her own broom, mop, and bucket. "Hi, I'm Lucy, and I'm here to help," she sang out cheerfully. Looking at her broom and mop, I knew she was serious. What a wonderful beginning to a friendship. And what a great friendship it has been. Through the years, even though we have moved across country, Lucille has always been with us for the major events of our lives.

A Friend with a Darning Needle

"I would like to make you an offer," Louise Stewart said. "I know you are busy as a wife, mother, and schoolteacher. I'm retired now and have time to do what I enjoy. I would enjoy doing the mending for your family. My mother taught me to sew when I was a young girl. I enjoy it and I am good at it, if I do say so myself. Would that be a help to you?"

"More than you know," I replied. "My mother never taught me to sew. She always said it was easier to do it herself, and she did the mending for our family until she died a few months ago. Would I ever be grateful for your help!"

Those stories tell how two special friendships began in my life. These women made it easy for me to respond. They showed an interest in me as a person and offered to help, no strings attached. We were off to a flying start, and our joyous relationships have lasted throughout our lives.

Concern Yourself More with Giving Than Receiving

Ted Engstrom, in his book, *The Fine Art of Friendship*, gives this advice: Make your friends number one, preferring them above yourself. Don't be like the woman who said to the old potbelly stove, "Come on, give me some warmth and then I'll add the wood." It doesn't work that way for stoves or people or friendship.

When you find yourself more concerned with giving than receiving, you will discover that friendships are more likely to happen. Yes, friendship does a lot for us, but no one likes to feel as though she is being used. If a person senses you wish her to be a friend so your needs will be met, her feelings of being manipulated will hinder a relationship from forming. If the message you give is that you like her as a person, that you enjoy being with her and you can be counted on to give a hand when needed, you have opened the door for a relationship to grow.

How to Show Your Interest in People

Dr. Paul Tournier wrote, "You can make more friends in two months by becoming interested in other people than you can in two years trying to get other people interested in you." How do you show your interest in other people? There are many ways, but the most important single thing to do is to listen. Not talk, but listen.

Listening is a skill that takes work. Talking comes naturally. In a conversation, most people look for an opening to add what they have to say. Sometimes it becomes a contest to see who can dominate the conversation. Most often when a person feels a need to talk more than to listen, it betrays the desire to impress the others present. Expressing your views, telling your stories, and giving your opinions can be a way of showing off, and showing off is a surefire way to turn other people off.

Active listening indicates an interest in the other person. Active listening is filled with responses, such as, "Really?" "Tell me more." "What happened next?" "How did that make you feel?" Good questions draw the speaker out and help her tell her story. Poor questions interrupt the story line or get the speaker sidetracked on some other issue. The worst questions are those that are asked to embarrass the speaker or to show they do not know as much about the subject as you do.

Learn the art of asking "the second question." The first question may show polite interest. An example might be, "How is your daughter?"

The answer may come, "She left for college last Monday."

It would be acceptable to reply, "Fine," and go on to the next subject. How much better to ask the second question. It could be, "What college? What is she interested in studying?" Even better might be the second question that shows an interest in your friend herself. That could be, "How are you making the adjustment to the empty nest?" The second question shows you heard, really heard what the other person was saying and that you are genuinely interested.

A Friend Listens

One Sunday morning after church Hazel hurried over to me. "How are you, Marilynn?" she asked.

"Not so good," I replied honestly. "I've just gotten the report from the doctor, and I'm about to have surgery."

"Congratulations!" she exclaimed. "I'm working on the menu for the women's luncheon coming up in two weeks. Would you like to bring your famous salad?"

"Because of my surgery I won't be able to be there," I replied.

"Oh, Marilynn, you keep too busy. One of these days you've just got to slow down. I'll ask Peggy for the salad then.

Do try to make the next meeting." Hazel headed across the church for Peggy, while I stood there in shock. I was hurting, concerned about my coming hospitalization, but all Hazel had heard was that I was going to miss the next meeting. Why I was going to miss was of no importance to her. It seemed the only thing that mattered was that she would be inconvenienced by having to ask someone else to prepare the salad.

I must admit I struggled with my feelings about Hazel. I thought we were friends, but I felt totally rejected by her response. I tried to make excuses for Hazel, telling myself she hadn't really heard what I had said. *But doesn't a friend listen when you tell her you are going to have an operation?* I thought.

Friends are too valuable to lose, so I worked out my relationship with Hazel, even though I was deeply hurt at the time. But I have found it takes less time to keep a friend than to make a new friend. Friendships grow as we work through problems together.

There is a glue that holds friendships together. A person must have adequate self-esteem to be a friend. Then she must accept the other person for who she is. There must be reciprocity. Friends have a right to put expectations upon each other as long as these demands are not possessive or excessive. Friends must be available. They need to take the opportunity to be together, or if separated, to write or telephone. Especially when support is needed, a true friend takes time to be there. We are more candid and open with friends than we are with others. A commitment to keep confidences is always there.

Make new friends but keep the old. They are your best investment in life.

TWELVE

Give the Gift of Encouragement

A sweet old lady encourages. A grumpy old grouch criticizes.

Encouragement has the power to change a woman's life.

Dorothy McKinney was content. She had a meaningful job as a practical nurse at Miami's Jackson Memorial Hospital. Although it was demanding at times, she found working with the patients to be rewarding and enjoyed her contacts with the people on the medical staff. She felt she had found her niche. Her co-workers appreciated her as a practical nurse but recognized that she could do more. They encouraged her to go on and take training to be a registered nurse.

"I was just doing a job, but others saw potential," Dorothy said. After seven years as a practical nurse, she began her studies to become a registered nurse. When she graduated, her friends continued to encourage her. In time she became supervisor of the orthopedics and neurology sections. She was surprised to receive the 1983 Outstanding Nurse Award and to be interviewed by national magazines. "All this is the result of the encouragement of other people," Dorothy happily points out. Whom do you know that might bloom beautifully where she is planted if you give her encouragement?

A Wife's Greatest Gift

Nate suffered a devastating blow when he lost his job. His boss had spoken curtly, "Your services are no longer needed." Nate left the building, a broken man, filled with despair. By the time he reached home, he was in a deep depression. When he entered his house, he blurted out to his wife, Sophia, "I lost my job. I am a complete, utter failure." A tense silence followed. Then a smile crept across Sophia's face. "What great news!" she responded. "Now you can write the book you have always wanted to write."

"But I have no job and no prospect of a job," he objected, completely without hope. "If I struggle to be an author, what would we live on? Where would the money come from?"

Sophia took her husband by the hand and led him to her kitchen. Opening a drawer, she took out a box that was hidden in the back. There was a horde of cash. Nate was overwhelmed. "Where on earth did you get this?" he gasped. "Whom does it belong to?"

"It's ours!" Sophia replied. "I always knew you were a man of genius. I knew one day you would become a great writer if only you were given the chance. Every week, out of the money you gave me for housekeeping, I have saved as much as I could so you would have your chance. Now there is enough to last us one whole year."

What a surprise! What encouragement! What a wife! Nathaniel Hawthorne did write that year, and the novel he wrote became one of the literary masterpieces of the Western Hemisphere. The book is *The Scarlet Letter.*

Do you see yourself as an encourager? Most of us would like to be. I asked a friend if she is an encourager. "I'm a realist," she responded, "but with my children and my husband, most of the time I find myself telling them what not to do! I guess I would have to admit I'm more critical than encouraging." So many of us would agree. We're convinced it's our job to keep our family and friends on the straight and narrow path.

It is easier to complain and criticize than to encourage, but encouragement pays far greater dividends.

A Surprising One-Day Fast

One morning Catherine Marshall felt the Lord had given her an assignment: For one day she was to go on a fast. Not a fast from food. This day she was to fast from criticism. She was not to criticize anyone about anything.

Immediately she began to make excuses. Wasn't it a part of being a Christian to make value judgments? Shouldn't she let others know what she thought was right and wrong? But the still, small voice insisted, *Just obey me without questioning. Go on an absolute fast on any critical statements for this day.*

Catherine had considered herself to be a positive person, but this morning as she attempted to keep from uttering any critical statements, she was surprised at how many judgmental thoughts entered her mind. Lunch turned out to be especially difficult. Her husband, mother, son, and secretary discussed school prayer, abortion, and the ERA amendment, subjects about which Catherine had strong opinions. Time and again barbed comments about certain leaders were on the tip of Catherine's tongue, but trying to be faithful, she did not utter a critical word. Near the end of lunch she observed to herself, with a degree of humor, that no one had even noticed her lack of critical comments. Even more, it was clear the federal government, the judicial system, and the church were able to get along very well without her penetrating observations.

It wasn't until afternoon that she was able to see that her fast on criticism was actually accomplishing something. Catherine began to pray about a concern she had had for years. She realized her prayers had been too negative and judgmental about the person for whom she was praying. Fasting from criticism meant fasting from criticism in her prayers, too! She began to pray in love, looking for every way to be positive as she prayed for this person and situation. Suddenly a whole new vision of possibilities for that life filled her mind, and with it the mark of the Holy Spirit—joy!

Next, ideas began to flow in a way she had not experienced in years. It became clear to her that her judgmental thoughts and spoken criticisms had not corrected one of the multitudinous problems she had been concerned with. "What it had done," Catherine said, "was to stifle my own creativity—in prayer, in relationships, perhaps even in writing—ideas God wanted to give me."

Catherine belonged to a prayer group, and at their next meeting, she shared about her day-long fast. The response was startling. One by one those in the group admitted that being critical was one of the major problems. It affected their marriages, their children, their work, and their relationships. One shared, "'Judge not' is translated 'Do not criticize' in Moffat's translation."

Compliments and Criticisms: Ten to One

We need to encourage more and criticize less. Too often we think one word of encouragement will balance out one word of criticism. Not so! We are more affected by criticism than by praise. We remember the words of censure that others speak, and we are sure they mean every word. We tend to forget words of praise or dismiss them as just polite conversation. We believe the harsh criticism but discount the nice things others say about us. It takes about ten compliments to offset one criticism, Dr. James Dobson observes. With so many critical people in the world, we need to major at being encouragers.

Although almost everyone would agree that encouragement is important, most people have very poor skills in this area. We know how to discourage. No one needs to teach us how to criticize. When encouragement is needed, we often do not know where to start and what to say.

Rudolph Dreikurs, in his helpful book, *Psychology in the Classroom*, points out that we must first observe how a person responds to our "encouragement." The same words spoken to two different people may encourage one and discourage the other. For instance, suppose you tell a woman she has great potential. Jane might be encouraged and take your words to mean that she has performed well and has real ability. As a result, she works harder to reach her potential. Mary might be discouraged when you tell her she has great potential. She could think it is a polite way to tell her she has not done as well as she can do. Especially if she has worked hard on her project, she might be tempted to give up.

Paul Welter, psychologist and author of *How to Help a Friend*, points out that urging is not always the same as encouragement. Urging often creates resistance. A person may feel she is being pushed into making a decision. Another word for repeated urging is *nagging*. While we may have the best intentions, persistent urging is usually perceived as being negative, while encouragement is always positive. Encouragement shows love. The encourager demonstrates her belief in people and seeks to inspire them to do their best and feel good about the choice.

Encourage the Dream

Dreams are a part of the process of making decisions, deciding what we should do, and setting goals for our life. Talking with another about our dreams is an important part of developing our vision for the future. The sweet old lady has learned the art of encouraging dreams. Too often, when a person begins to share her dream, she is told her ideas are stupid or impossible. Children and young people often find this to be true when they talk about their future. What should you do when someone's dream seems impractical or unrealistic?

Richard Dortch, in his book *Caring Enough to Help the One You Love*, gives a helpful example. Suppose your son watches the video of the movie, *Raiders of the Lost Ark*, and rushes in to tell you he wants to become an archaeologist. What do you say? You could respond, "Being an archaeologist is nothing like you see in the movies. First you have to have a college degree, and archaeology is a tough subject. And when you do go to work, it won't be exciting. You may be out in the desert sun, digging for months at a time. Maybe you'll never find anything important. Besides, you'll never make any money being an archaeologist. Don't expect us to support you for the rest of your life! Why would you want to waste your life that way?"

That kind of response will dash a dream into a million pieces on the kitchen floor. It will rob a child of the exhilaration of having a dream and most likely teach him or her it is not safe to share their hopes and dreams again.

What response would an encourager give that would still be realistic? "That's interesting, Son. You've always liked history, and I can see that you would think digging up the past would be exciting. Why don't you save up for a subscription to an archaeology magazine or maybe the *National Geographic?* You can look them over at the library and see if that is a career you would like to have. Maybe on one of our vacations we could go to a historical dig and see how they do it."

Guidance is given without crushing the excitement of the dream. The mother has been realistic but not demeaning or insensitive. The son will feel free to talk more about what he would like to do with his life and to share other dreams. He will feel that his mother listened to what he had to say, validated his enthusiasm, believed in his abilities, and will be willing to explore possibilities with him.

Encouragers Warm the Soul

My husband and I had a wonderful evening as we planned this chapter. We began to recall the people through the years who had encouraged us. My first remembrance was of my grandmother Emma. In my early childhood she called me her little songbird and encouraged me to sing. Together Bill and I remembered family and friends whose words had helped us. We were surprised at how many people there were. We were a little chagrined that we had not remembered more often these good folks whose words and letters had meant so much to us. We were surprised at how many of the encouragers were plain, ordinary people who probably had no inkling of how important they had been to us. Our hearts were warmed as we spent the evening hours reminiscing about the people whose encouragement had been so important in our lives. I am certain everyone has had the blessing of persons who have given encouragement. It will be a special time for you, and it will brighten even the darkest day if you take time to recall the words of encouragement that others gave to you.

When to Encourage

People need to be encouraged at all times. Here are a few illustrations. Volunteers need encouragement. One of our good friends is a talented musician who played the organ for her church for many years. She did this as a willing act of service as a volunteer. Through rain and snow she was there. Often when she was feeling sick, she still made the effort. She missed many family gatherings and other events because every Sunday she faithfully played for the Sunday services. During the week she took time to practice with the choir and soloists. It was a sacrifice of love to her Lord. Did the congregation care? Often a year would go by without a single person stopping to say thank-you or tell how he or she enjoyed the playing. What a difference a word of encouragement would have made.

Look for volunteers. You will find them everywhere. Often they receive criticism and complaints on a regular basis but few words of appreciation. When I stop at the hospital information desk to ask directions to a patient's room, I thank the volunteer for spending a part of her day to help me. It's fun to ask what she would be doing if she were not volunteering. Most of the volunteers are busy people who make a real effort to give of themselves to help others.

The people who are paid for their services need encouragement too. This is especially true of those who work hard and often are paid very little. For example, in most states, preschool teachers are required to be highly educated, take many specialized courses, and spend time practice-teaching under supervision before they receive their credentials, yet they are often paid minimum wage. Of course, they do it because they love children. Caring for children is one of the most important tasks in the world, but it is also difficult. How they need encouragement.

A person who is new to a group or community needs encouragement. Churches often consider themselves to be friendly, and they are. But often they are friendly only to their friends. When my husband was the administrator of a retirement home, he would encourage the residents to begin to attend a church. The response he received most often was, "You don't know how hard it is to go someplace by yourself for the first time." I decided I would try it for myself. Instead of attending my regular church, I attended a good church with a fine reputation. Conversation flowed, hugs and warmth abounded. As a stranger, I was greeted by the usher at the door, but no one else took time to notice me. When I slipped into a pew, the others looked at me as if to say, "Who are you?" There were no smiles, and I took their looks to mean, "What are you doing here?" The bulletin said coffee and fellowship were to follow the service. I went hopefully. I poured myself a cup of coffee. It seemed very awkward to break into one of the circles of conversation. I knew I had the skills to initiate contacts there if I wanted to work at it, but I realized many people would not. They would see the friendly circles as being closed to outsiders. I tried other churches. To my surprise, once I passed the "official" greeters, I was ignored in many churches.

People need encouragement when life is hard. We often respond well when a person is in the hospital, but if they return home for a long recuperation it is easy to forget them. When a long illness besets someone, the needs of the caregiver are usually overlooked. Cards and flowers are sent to the one who is sick or shut in. The caregiver sometimes is under an even greater strain but is largely forgotten. When I send a card to a shut-in, I like to send a separate note of love and appreciation to the caregiver as well.

People should be encouraged when they give of their time and talent. For a time, my husband was the interim pastor of a very small church. This church regularly had outstanding soloists come and sing. Why were the musicians who normally sing in large churches willing to donate their time and talent to such a small audience? Because the members of this small congregation went out of their way to express their appreciation. Many of the singers told my husband that they often felt taken for granted by their large home church. Although hundreds of people were present for worship, sometimes not even one would comment on the solo they had sung. The soloists were willing to come to a small church where the people eagerly expressed appreciation, told them what their ministry in music meant to them, and encouraged them to continue to use their gifts.

How surprising that many people think that a capable person who does well needs no confirmation. They assume the person is aware she has done a good job and does not need their encouragement. Everyone needs encouragement! As a minister's wife, I have had many women who have worked faithfully ask me, "Does anybody care?" Speak up; let people know you have appreciated their contribution.

Include Your Family

Be as kind to your family as you are to others. Let them know you believe in them and that they have your support. Notice successes, however small. Be their cheerleader, and like a good cheerleader, come be their support even more when the going gets tough. Genuine love results in encouragement.

What Do People Call You?

One of my favorite biblical characters is a man named Joseph. We read in Acts 4 that the people in his home church had a special name for him. They nicknamed him Barnabas, which means *the encourager*. Little wonder! When some of the members of the church in Jerusalem were having a difficult time financially, without being asked, Barnabas sold some of his property to help them. The Jewish Christians in Jerusalem became concerned when they heard the non-Jewish people in Antioch were becoming Christians, so they sent Barnabas to look into the matter. Barnabas found the Christians in Antioch to have a valid faith even though they had different customs. What do you do with people who are different from you? Barnabas encouraged them. Church historians credit him and his encouragement of the Christians in Antioch as being the turning point in Christianity. Up to this point, all the Christians were Jewish. After this, Christianity spread throughout all the world.

Saul of Tarsus was the enemy of the church, arresting many of the Christians and sending them to prison. He was present at the stoning of Stephen. On the Damascus Road, Saul had a conversion experience. He became a Christian and was given a new name, Paul. Peter, James, and John and most other Christians did not believe that Paul was a genuine Christian. It was Barnabas who encouraged Paul and persuaded the others to accept him.

Barnabas encouraged Paul to go with him on the first missionary journey. They took Barnabas's young cousin, John Mark, along with them. We are not told why, but John Mark quit and went home. What do you do with a quitter? Someone who fails? Paul didn't ever want to take him along again on a missionary journey. But Barnabas encouraged the young man. Paul went alone on the next missionary journey, but Barnabas took John Mark with him to spread the Gospel in another direction. The story has a surprise ending. Encouragement works! Today we remember John Mark as Mark, the inspired writer of the gospel according to Mark.

I encourage you to join the Royal Society of Encouragers. Let's choose Barnabas to be our patron saint.

THIRTEEN

✿

More Than Random Acts of Kindness

A sweet old lady is kind. A grumpy old grouch is selfish.

*T*ry it. You'll like it! When doing your grocery shopping, purchase a package of chewing gum, then give it as a gift to the cashier at the checkout. On a hot day, give a cold can of Coke to the garbage collector when he picks up your trash. Drop a coin in a stranger's parking meter that is about to expire.

You see it on bumper stickers: PRACTICE RANDOM ACTS OF KINDNESS. What are random acts of kindness? The good folk who advocate this practice define them as unexpected, unrequired, thoughtful actions that will brighten another's day. They will brighten your day, too. Part of the fun is to see the reaction on someone's face when he or she is caught by surprise by an unexpected, warmhearted deed. The astonishment is usually the greatest when the recipient of a random act of kindness is caught off guard by a total stranger.

The idea was the brainchild of Anne Herbert, a writer in Marin County, California. For days she had been thinking about how violence seemed to be escalating everywhere. Could something positive be done to counteract this trend? Could an underground movement be started to promote kindness instead? *If you think there should be more of something, do it—randomly,* she thought. *Kindness can build on itself as much as violence can.* Being a writer, she knew the importance of words. Could she find the right phrase that would express the idea in a way that people would not only remember but also be inspired to action? After mulling over the idea for days, it suddenly came to her when she was in a restaurant. She took out her pen and wrote on a place mat: *Practice random acts of kindness and senseless acts of beauty.*

The idea was born. The catchy phrase began to take on a life of its own and spread like wildfire, often without any organized effort. Someone would place it on a bulletin board at a factory; others would copy it and place it on the refrigerator in their home or in their church newsletter. Teachers would write the phrase on blackboards at school. Salesmen added the words to their business cards. People included the idea in the letters they wrote. It popped up on radio and television talk shows and on bumper stickers everywhere. There were articles in the *Ladies' Home Journal, Woman's Day, Family Circle,* and other magazines. Even the *Reader's Digest* carried an article on the conspiracy of kindness.

I Remember When

Some of my fondest memories are of the times when I was the recipient of an unexpected act of kindness. My love of angels began when I was a small girl, but few people paid any attention. My Sunday school teacher did! On my birthday, Miss Nelson made me an angel food cake. Not only that, but she found a birthday card that had an angel on it. Inside it said, "To an angel like you." The years have passed, but I have never forgotten that unexpected act that brought such validation to a young girl. Each time I remember, I am flooded with warmth, even though it happened many years ago.

Baking pies has never been my thing. One Christmas when I was a young mother, a friend, Mary Edith Gore, who lived twenty miles away, left a package for me. When I opened it, I found a dozen jars of home-canned fruits with a cryptic note that the rest of my gift was in the coldest place in town. A few hours later another friend rang our doorbell. "Mary Edith left this in our freezer and asked me to deliver it to you today," she said. She handed me a package wrapped in freezer paper. Inside were a dozen frozen homemade pie shells. What a neat surprise! We enjoyed that unexpected gift a dozen times as we had pie for dessert, but we have enjoyed the memory a hundred times in the years that have passed.

I enjoy doing random acts of kindness. It builds my self-esteem, and I feel more human. Try it and see if you don't see yourself as being gracious, good, nice, decent, warmhearted, and compassionate when you reach out and touch another.

I have a friend who has been captured by the concept of random acts of kindness. It was a totally new idea to her, and she throws herself into it with all the zeal that a new convert brings to her religion. From time to time she finds the opportunity to surprise an unsuspecting stranger with a serendipitous act; then she delights to recount the incident to any who will listen, exhorting them to join in the crusade to practice random acts of kindness. "It's a wonderful new concept," she enthusiastically proclaims. "It's one of the greatest ideas that has come along in our time."

It is a wonderful idea to do deeds of kindness. It is hardly new, however. For decades the Boy Scout motto has been "Do a good deed daily." The motto was based on the commonly held value that being kind and helpful is a virtue that everyone should embrace and that we should begin to develop this habit when we are children. The idea is centuries old. Jesus taught, "Be kind to one another." This is one of the first Bible verses little children are taught in Sunday school. It is a lesson we are to apply throughout our lives.

Practice Random Acts of Kindness

Anne Herbert conceives of this as an underground movement, where ordinary people engage in guerrilla goodness, doing simple acts of kindness and civility. If enough people commit themselves to this ideal, possibly that generosity and thoughtfulness can become the norm, and our world will become a little kinder and gentler. To get you started, here are some good deeds you can do to brighten the lives of those around you:

- Call a sick friend.
- Write a note of appreciation to your child's teacher.
- Thank your mail carrier. In the post office ask for the form to make a written commendation.
- Smile more often.
- Send a greeting card to a child.
- Call a friend from the past "I was just remembering the good times we shared."
- Put a joke or riddle in your child's lunch box.
- Give a compliment to the checker in the grocery store.
- Call your pastor in the middle of the week to tell him his sermon was helpful.
- Give an understanding, sympathetic look to a mother with a screaming child.
- Visit an elderly relative.
- When your spouse is in the shower, warm his towel in the dryer.
- Look for the good in a problem child and compliment him.
- Organize a friendship lunch and ask everyone to bring a favorite food.
- When you are about to criticize, stop and find a compliment you can give instead.

Don't just choose one of the above. The possibilities are endless. The best ideas are ones that fit your situation. Make it your aim always to be looking for ways to slip a little kindness into an ordinary day. At times this will be difficult. The people around you may be rude, demanding, and thoughtless. That's when you are really needed. Don't let the grinches win!

Remember, you are a part of the secret underground using guerrilla tactics to replace harshness with kindness. Think of words you can speak or quiet deeds you can do to change the atmosphere.

Fools Rush In

We humans have a way of spoiling even good ideas. Every cause has a few misguided fanatics who turn others off by their overzealous attempts to do something good but do it in the wrong way or because of wrong motives. That's why it's important to consider a few ground rules before rushing out to join the kindness revolution.

Random acts can never replace consistent kindness. It may be an improvement for a person who is usually rude to do a few random acts of kindness. Unfortunately it may lull her into complacency, and she may begin to think of herself as a nice, caring person, while those around her are crippled by her insensitivity. One woman prides herself on her Tinkerbell efforts at spreading a sprinkling of fairy dust of kindness to make strangers feel better. She seldom sees her invalid mother and almost never offers to help her older sister who cares for their mother constantly. Random acts of kindness make it easy to fool ourselves into thinking we are doing something meaningful, when what we are doing may be avoiding a commitment to our real responsibilities. We need to add random acts of kindness to a lifestyle that is consistently thoughtful and caring.

We need to be sincere. Coming out of the supermarket, I noticed a woman stopping a customer who was hurrying to her car with a full basket of groceries. "You are so unique; you're extraordinary!" she exclaimed. Then she rushed over to me. "You are so unique; you're extraordinary!" she insisted, then turned to find someone else to whom she could deliver the identical message. I was a total stranger. She had no way of knowing if I was special, helpful, funny, caring, loving, or giving. Was anyone helped as she repeated the same six words to any and all who passed by? Our words and deeds need to be sincere; otherwise, they may have the opposite effect, and we come off as being phony.

We need to respect personal boundaries. People have different comfort levels. Most people like to be hugged. I know others who are offended if their space is violated. They consider hugging to be an act of intimacy that should only be performed by a few special people in their lives—and I know one who doesn't want to be hugged by anyone! If you are a hugger, that doesn't mean you should stop hugging. Just don't force it on those who are unwilling.

It is not always kind to help another person. I remember when my daughter was little how she would often say, "Mother, I can do it myself!" Some people like to be helped. Others want to do things themselves. Take time to learn each person's preference. One person may appreciate it if you bring her a cup of coffee. She may think it's great you noticed she uses both cream and sugar and that you prepared it that way for her. Another person may prefer to get her own coffee and be sure it has just the exact amount of sugar and cream she prefers.

This is especially true of people with handicaps. Some delight in receiving special treatment. Others are proud of their independence and are happiest when they can take care of themselves. Some are sensitive and do not want attention drawn to themselves and their handicap.

The Mission Inn is a famous historical landmark hotel in my hometown of Riverside, California. Many of the rich and famous have been entertained there. Richard and Pat Nixon were married in its beautiful chapel. The Ronald Reagans spent their first night together in the honeymoon suite. Years earlier President Taft planned a visit to Mission Inn. The innkeeper, Frank Miller, had his craftsmen build a special chair for the president. The workmanship was excellent and it was superbly carved. Because the president was very large and very heavy, the chair was also very large. Frank Miller had planned it with the best of motives to show his thoughtfulness in preparing for a presidential visit. President Taft was not pleased. He was sensitive about his weight, and he thought the oversized chair drew unneeded attention to his girth. He was right! The chair stands now in the lobby of the historic Mission Inn. The docents point with pride to the craftsmanship with which the chair was made, but after a tour of the inn, the main attraction the visitors remember is how large a man President Taft was. It reminds us that when we plan our acts of kindness, we need to be thoughtful of the feelings of others.

It is not kindness if the receiver does not want our act of kindness. Remember the classic story of the Boy Scout who helped the little old lady to cross the street, only to discover she did not want to cross the street? Too often, random acts can bring pleasure to the one doing the act but may not be helpful or pleasing to the recipient of the act.

The spirit is more important than the act. We need to be sensitive, never patronizing as we do acts of kindness. If a person feels we are talking down to him, our words will not bring encouragement and cheer. If we act superior, it will cancel out the good we hope to do.

The right motive is important. While it is true that an act of kindness can bring joy and healing to us, our primary motive should be to give unselfishly to another. The best acts of kindness are those that are gifts of grace, given without requiring gratitude in return. If we cannot give without feelings of resentment, it is better not to give. We should do our acts of kindness unconditionally. If possible, do them anonymously, just because it is the right thing to do.

Accept the kindness of others. While it is more blessed to give than to receive, it should be a blessing to receive as well. Others can not be blessed by giving if we are unwilling to receive. A single mother worked long hours so that her daughter would be able to attend college. The daughter appreciated the sacrifices her mother was making and was very frugal in her lifestyle. As Christmas approached, the daughter wanted to show her love and tried to plan a Christmas gift for her mother that would show her gratefulness. She noticed how worn and wrinkled her mother's hands had become as a result of her many hours of work. The daughter decided to give her mother a nice pair of gloves to wear to church. To have the money to buy the gloves, the daughter went without one meal each day and saved the money until she had the purchase price of the gloves. On Christmas Day she lovingly gave her gift to her mother who had sacrificed so much for her. The mother refused the gift, saying with anger, "Return those gloves to the store and get your money back. I'm not working hard so you will be able to buy extravagant gifts!"

The girl was crushed. Her mother's unwillingness to accept a sacrificial gift kept the daughter from experiencing the joy of giving. How much more blessed it would have been if the mother had been willing to receive as well as to give.

Be kind to others by allowing them to be kind to you.

Remember Always to Be Kind

Practice random acts of kindness. Especially today when our society has so much selfishness and so many mean-spirited people, we need those who will be giving and who will forget the gift. In the face of rudeness we need to be polite. While some are violent, we need to model a kinder, gentler spirit. Random acts of kindness are a good place to begin. Random acts of kindness can serve as an excellent reminder that we always need a spirit of love, and kindness should be our consistent way of life. Remember the words of Jesus, "Be kind to one another."

FOURTEEN

❦❧

Forgiveness

*A sweet old lady forgives. A grumpy old grouch
holds grudges.*

The miracle of forgiveness is illustrated in the true story of
a six-year-old girl who mystified Harvard child psychiatrist, Dr. Robert Coles. Coles studied the lives of children and
eventually received a Pulitzer prize for his multivolume work,
Children of Crisis.

In 1960 Dr. Coles saw a mob of people standing and
screaming outside the William T. Franz Elementary School in
New Orleans. It was two o'clock in the afternoon. "What's happening?" the psychiatrist asked.

"She's coming out in a half hour," they answered.

"Who is coming out?" Dr. Coles asked.

The crowd answered, shouting cuss words and foul language. Dr. Coles decided to wait and see what was happening.
He did not have long to wait. A six-year-old black girl escorted
by two federal marshals came out of Franz School. This was
the moment the crowd was waiting for. They called the little
girl unspeakable names. They hurled curses at her from their
snarling lips. They threatened her with violence and yelled
they would kill her. The tumult continued until the federal marshals bundled the first grader into a car and drove away. No
one else came out of the school.

The U.S. Supreme Court had ordered that public schools should be desegregated, and a federal judge had pressured New Orleans all-white schools to admit black students. The lone black student to attend Franz School was Ruby Bridges. The day she came to first grade, all the other students refused to attend.

Dr. Coles' specialty is children under stress. Here was a girl that was under tremendous stress. He made arrangements to meet with Ruby Bridges' family and to see the first grade child twice a week.

He would begin with the questions a child psychiatrist asks when probing for evidence of turmoil. "How are you doing, Ruby?"

"I'm okay."

"Mrs. Bridges, how is Ruby doing?"

"She's doing fine."

"Is she sleeping okay?"

"Yes, Ruby is sleeping fine."

"Are you sure?"

"Yes."

"Well, how's Ruby's appetite?"

"It's fine."

"How do you think Ruby is doing with her friends when she comes home from school?"

"Ruby's fine when she comes home. She plays, and sometimes she reads the books she brings home from school. She's in first grade and just learning how to read."

"Does Ruby seem upset at any time?"

"No, Ruby doesn't seem too upset," answered Mrs. Bridges.

Day after day Ruby faced the jeering, taunting mob before and after school. Dr. Coles continued to see Ruby and her parents twice a week for several months. He talked to Ruby's schoolteacher. "I don't understand this child," she said. "She seems so happy. She comes here so cheerfully."

One night Dr. Coles went to the Bridges' home. "Ruby, how was your day today?"

She replied, "It was okay."

"I was talking to your teacher today, and she told me she saw you talking to the people in the street."

"I wasn't talking to them. I was just saying a prayer for them."

"Ruby, do you pray for the people out there?"

"Oh, yes."

"Why do you do that?"

"Because they need praying for," she answered.

"But Ruby, I'm puzzled. Why should you be the one to pray for such people, given what they do to you twice a day, five days a week?"

"Well," she said, "especially it should be me." Then she told the psychiatrist that Jesus went through a lot of trouble, too, and he prayed, "Father, forgive them because they don't know what they are doing."

Little Ruby kept praying, day after day, on the streets of New Orleans for a year. The psychiatrist monitored her closely. He was mystified. Here was a child under tremendous stress who was happy and well-adjusted. The textbooks on psychiatry had no explanation. What was Ruby Bridges' secret?

Ruby trusted God. She forgave. She prayed for those who would be her enemies.

Is Forgiveness Hard for You?

I admire Ruby Bridges. She was able to forgive even in the most difficult circumstances. I know this is right, but the ability to forgive that came easily and naturally to Ruby is more difficult for most of us. For some it even appears to be impossible.

Although this may be the most important chapter in this book, in many ways it has been the most difficult chapter for me to write. I am one of those persons for whom forgiveness does not come easily. I know what it is like to be hurt deeply, because I have experienced it. Some wounds from the past are so personal that even now, although I have been able to forgive, I cannot go public with the details. The principles of forgiveness I share are those I have learned in the cauldron of experience. Too often, I have been a slow learner. As a result, I have learned firsthand the painful consequences of allowing the root of bitterness to grow, the inevitable result of the lack of forgiveness. Therefore, I am convinced that nothing in life except love is more important than forgiveness, and love cannot exist without forgiveness.

Has someone hurt you and you cannot forget it? Perhaps it was yesterday. Maybe it was a lifetime ago. It was a hurt you did not deserve; it lodged deep in your memory and keeps on hurting you now.

You are not alone. This is a universal human condition. We live in a world where people do hurt each other. The sad truth is that even well-meaning people sometimes wound those they love. The more we open ourselves to love, the more we become vulnerable to another's disloyalty or even betrayal. Others who are not friends deliberately cause us grief.

Fortunately, every unkindness does not have dire consequences. Slights we soon forget; indeed some we choose to ignore. Others burrow deep into our souls, grow like a silent cancer, and erupt with an unexpected bitterness when we least expect it. Deep hurts from our past, hurts we never deserved, invade us now and rob us of our joy. We long for the ability to turn back the calendar and eliminate the event from our life. If only that painful moment had never happened! But the pains of the past are as relentless as the ocean tides. They keep coming, over and over, and there seems to be nothing we can do about it.

Nothing?

Hannah Arendt, the respected philosopher grapples with this problem in her book, *The Human Condition*. Her conclusion is that there is only one way to keep painful memories from returning over and over again. She calls it the "faculty of forgiveness."

Do you remember the day in 1984 when Pope John Paul II went to the Rebibbia Prison in Rome to visit Mehmet Ali Agca?

This was the man who had tried to kill him. Now the pope sought him out. His message was, "I forgive you." *TIME* magazine reported, "As Pope John Paul tenderly held the hand that had held the gun that was meant to kill him—it was a startling drama of forgiveness and reconciliation."

The picture of the pope forgiving his would-be assassin was on the front page of newspapers around the world. It was a dramatic moment. It was the right thing, the Christian thing, to do. Could you have done that? Would you? Perhaps it was easier for the pope to do because he is a professional forgiver, and he knew the whole world was watching. I would not take one iota of credit away from the pope, but I would point out that for us ordinary people it may be a thousand times harder to forgive and forget when no one is watching.

Webster's Dictionary gives this definition for *forgive:* "to give up resentment against, or the desire to punish; stop being angry with; pardon."

When Forgiveness Is Easy

Our book, *A Rustle of Angels*, was nominated for a print media award given by the Excellence in Media Foundation. The award ceremony was held in the famed Hollywood Roosevelt Hotel where the Oscars were originally given. Many of the rich and famous as well as television and movie stars attended the dinner and ceremony. It was an exciting night for us. Our table was filled with friends, some who had come from a distance, to celebrate with us if we won an angel award and console us if we lost. Before the ceremony as we mingled with the media and celebrities in the press room, Mary Dorr, the founder of the Angel Awards, confided to us that the judges had been unanimous and our book was a winner. We were overjoyed.

We enjoyed the elegant dinner that preceded the ceremony. It was exciting to be there in person as the awards were given. *The Lion King* won the Sweepstakes Award. *Forrest Gump* received the award for best motion picture. *Christy* and *Touched By an Angel* were winners for television series. As the

awards continued to be given out, our excitement and anticipation increased. We kept waiting for our names to be called.
We waited in vain. The ceremonies ended, but there had been
no mention of our book, *A Rustle of Angels*, or its authors. We
had not received an award after all. I was crushed and disappointed. It hurt even more because we had been told we were
winners. It hurt to be left out, and I was embarrassed that it
happened in front of our friends. I was hurt, yes, and angry,
too. Sally, one of our friends who had come from Denver for
the occasion, said, "Marilynn, if this had happened to me, I
would just put my head down on the table and cry!" I tried to
keep my head up, but I was blinking back the tears.

As the hall began to empty, my husband and I looked for
Mary Dorr. I must admit I was having a hard time with my
churning emotions. I had gone from a high when I had heard
our book had been chosen as a winner to the lowest of lows
when it did not receive an award at all.

I found Mary Dorr, beautiful and composed, saying
farewell to the guests as they left. "Mary," I said, trying to keep
my voice from breaking, "did we win an award or didn't we?"

"Marilynn, you certainly did," Mary replied. "You were
scheduled to be given the print media award for *A Rustle of
Angels*."

"But what happened?" I asked.

"This year we hired a new company to produce the award
show. They made several mistakes that I discovered as the
show went on. One of them was that your award was not
included. I feel so terrible about it," Mary said. "I'm sorry, truly
sorry."

I knew she was sincere, but my heart was still breaking
into a thousand pieces. I thought, *How can I forgive those who
have been so neglectful and negligent? There will never be a
second chance to receive this award.*

But Mary sprang into action. She had one of the stagehands
go backstage and find the award. She led us to the podium

then called to the official photographer. We posed as Mary presented the award to us.

But it wasn't the same! It was true, we had our award, but we had missed the experience of the presentation during the ceremony. Mary seemed to read my mind.

"Marilynn," she said, "this year we are dividing the award ceremonies. In addition to tonight's presentation in Hollywood, we will also be having an awards ceremony for those on the East Coast. It will be held at Sardi's in New York City. You are invited, and I promise you we will make your presentation special there."

It was special. Our friends were not there to see it, but our daughter Sharon and her husband, Bob Scott, who had just won an Emmy Award, were there. The Excellence in Media Awards drew a dazzling array of people. Diane Sawyer was presented a major award for her work in television journalism. Helen Thomas, the reporter who covers the White House, was given a lifetime achievement award. In front of a packed house, our names were read and we were presented (officially) with a beautiful statuette of a silver angel.

This is a story of forgiveness. That night in the Hollywood Roosevelt Hotel I was bitterly disappointed. I was angry with those who had been inept. I was filled with resentment. It was a painful moment and I was hurt, a hurt I felt I did not deserve.

Forgiveness in this case was made easier by the graciousness of Mary Dorr. Although she was not personally responsible for the error, she sincerely apologized for the organization. She did what she could to make amends, first by presenting the award to us after the show, then by inviting us to the New York ceremonies. How could I help but love Mary when she did everything possible to make amends? It also helped that those who had made the errors were people we did not know and we would have no reason to associate with them later. (A different staff handled the New York presentations, where everything went beautifully.)

When Forgiveness Is Hard

How far more difficult to forgive when a person deliberately causes hurt, shows no remorse, and may even choose to sever a relationship. How heartbreaking to be betrayed by a friend when you are the innocent party. Grief results when you are ostracized by a group because someone spread lies about you. To be rejected by one's spouse in divorce can be more devastating than losing a partner in death. To be disowned by one's parents is a pain that can only be matched by rejection from one's children. Yet in all situations we are called to forgive.

Forgiveness is difficult when you receive a hurt you did not deserve from someone close to you. Forgiveness is more difficult to give when the offense was deliberate. It is extremely difficult to forgive when the person who offended you has no remorse and may even delight in your misery. The hurt can easily become hatred. You cannot shake the memory of it. The other person has become your enemy. You cannot wish him well, and you sometimes want him to suffer as you are suffering.

Yes, I would be willing to forgive, is what many think, *but first she must admit she is wrong, be genuinely repentant, say she is sorry, and ask for forgiveness.*

Should you forgive when a person does not seek your forgiveness? Or even acknowledge that she has done anything wrong? When the other person will not agree to set things right and restore the relationship? When she continues to hurt you deliberately again and again?

Yes.

Forgiveness is best when it results in healing, when it brings about reconciliation, and gives peace to both the offended and the offending person. In our imperfect world this does not always happen. Indeed, for many (most?) people some hurts go unresolved. Some grudges are carried through the years. Family members, former friends, and others remain unforgiven.

What happens when we do not forgive? Yes, a relationship is strained, if not broken. Sometimes not forgiving is a source of pain to the other person. It may be one way we have of punishing others for their actions. Sometimes this is a way of manipulating others to admit they were wrong and say they are sorry. But our bitterness and unforgiving spirit can have the opposite effect. The person we are angry with may withdraw and insulate herself from us. Or she may be driven away and all hope for reconciliation may be lost. Sometimes others react by fighting back, becoming more difficult, more hateful. Unforgiveness can make an enemy of another, causing him to look for a way to undermine you and cause you grief at every opportunity.

The personal cost is usually the highest. When we do not forgive, unresolved anger remains in our lives. If we allow ourselves to dwell on our hurts and injuries, bitterness develops. Harboring a spirit of unforgiveness results in hostility. This hostility is often expressed not only toward those who have caused us grief but also toward others we care about. Our refusal to forgive is actually a form of hatred. The sad fact is that hate seldom hurts the person it is directed at, but it always hurts the person who harbors it.

Unforgiveness can result in sleepless nights. A multitude of physical disorders can result, including headaches, colitis, ulcers, exhaustion, and even heart attacks. An unforgiving spirit robs us of our joy in living. It stifles our creativity and is one cause for depression.

Forgiveness may be hard, but it is much harder to live with the fruits of an unforgiving spirit. Forgiveness frees and heals. Unforgiveness, with its resentments and bitterness, continues to hurt, takes the bloom off life, and can lead to an early grave.

How Do I Forgive?

My friend Evelyn Christenson shared her personal experience with me, a portion of which is found in her book, *What Happens When We Pray for Our Families*. Evelyn has been a blessing to women the world over through her books and seminars on prayer beginning with *What Happens When Women*

Pray. I have found her to be one of the most genuine Christians I have met. However, her closeness to Christ does not keep her from being hurt by others. One day, quite unexpectedly, a terrible confrontation occurred in her family. A member of her extended family hurt her. It was unfair. It was undeserved. It was devastating.

Even though Evelyn was shattered, she had to leave almost immediately to fulfill an important speaking engagement at a college in a neighboring state. Fortunately, her husband, Chris, was there to drive her to the meeting two-and-a-half hours away. Evelyn climbed into the back of the van, realizing she was in no condition to minister to the audience that would be waiting. She tried to pray. "How do I pray when I am bleeding this hard?" she cried out to God. "Lord, what should I do? How should I handle this? Please give me the attitude you want me to have."

What can a person do when she is completely shattered? In her seminars Evelyn had taught the biblical principles of forgiveness to thousands of women. Now she was the one who needed God's help. It didn't lessen her anguish because she had taught about forgiveness. She was hurting badly. In fact, the undeserved pain was so bad it was difficult to forgive. But Evelyn knew she must. Unless she found peace, she could not possibly minister to the waiting audience. Unless she dealt with the problem, the bitterness would grow and affect all her relationships. Jesus teaches that we must forgive. She knew it was a sin, a clear disobedience if she refused to obey Christ's clear command. Evelyn focused on the formula for forgiveness from 2 Corinthians 2:5–11 that she had taught hundreds of times and had used in her personal life.

Lord, Change Me

Evelyn began to agonize in prayer, crying, "O Lord, change *me;* change *me!* Forgive me, Father, for everything that is my fault. Lord, make me absolutely clean before you!" She was not repeating words or a formula. It was a sincere, heartfelt prayer. "Lord, forgive me for retaliating verbally," she pleaded. "Cleanse me from my ugly reactions and un-Christlike attitudes." It was important to make her relationship with her heavenly Father right before she moved on to the business of forgiveness.

Lord, Help Me Forgive

To forgive, not just in words but truly in the heart, is a difficult process. Our human reaction is to get even. We need to be honest about our anger. We need God's help. We may need to pray, "Lord make me willing to be willing to forgive." Evelyn realized it would do no good for her to ask God to forgive her if she in turn was not willing to forgive others. She needed help doing it. She prayed, "Lord, help me to forgive." And with his help she did. She was able to forgive within hours after she had been hurt.

Lord, Help Me Comfort Those Who Hurt Me

The teaching about forgiveness in 2 Corinthians 2:7 goes further. "You ought to forgive and comfort him." Evelyn remembered the story of Joseph. He did not retaliate against the brothers who had treated him so meanly, even selling him into slavery. He had forgiven them. "Fear not," he said to them, calming their fears and talking kindly to them. Now God confirmed to Evelyn that even if family members continued to be contentious, she must speak kindly to them and avoid an attitude of retaliation. She considered each of the family members involved and resolved that her attitude toward them would be friendly and positive, never retaliatory. When this was done, the peace of God settled in around her.

Lord, Enable Me to Pray for Those Who Hurt Me

It's not enough to call a truce. When loved ones hurt us, we must pray for them, not just about them. Jesus said, "Love your enemies and pray for those who persecute you" (Matthew 5:44). Too many people pray asking God to get even for them and give the other person "what they deserve." God wants to work in our hearts until we are willing to pray for their good. Often this takes time.

Lord, Help Me Love

Evelyn remembered the words of our Lord, "Love your enemies and pray for those who persecute you" (Matthew 5:44). When a hurt is new and deep, it is difficult to love. That's why Evelyn found it necessary to pray, "Lord, help me love. Fill me with your love." Usually the results of this prayer are not instantaneous. God begins his work as soon as we pray, but often we need to continue to pray daily for our love to grow. When we make this a matter of prayer, we will discover ways to nurture love and help it grow.

Lord, Enable Us to Pray Together

Next, Evelyn prayed for the best outcome, that a time would come when the two of them would be able to pray together. Healing takes place when two Christians commit themselves and their situation to God, praying for forgiveness, a restoration of love, and the desire to do God's will. If it is possible, set up a time to pray with the person who has hurt you.

Of course, some would never consent to pray. Their anger may be too great, they may be too embarrassed, or they may not believe in prayer. Perhaps they may not even be willing to talk with you. If it is impossible or inadvisable to pray together, don't allow yourself the smug satisfaction of feeling spiritually superior. Instead, humbly ask God to help you with your part in the healing process.

Lord, Call Others to Pray for Me and Us

The intercessory prayers of others always help. At times when we are so shattered, it is difficult to pray. Words simply won't come. We need others to intercede and storm the gates of heaven for us. Evelyn knew her prayer partners were praying for her and that her prayer chains were praying. In this case they had no idea of her need or what had happened, but Evelyn gained strength knowing they were praying for her.

How Prayers Are Answered

Evelyn began the trip shattered, hurt, and angry. She was in no condition to talk to a group about the things of God. By the time she arrived, she had truly opened her heart to forgive. In doing so, she also found the peace of God. But she was exhausted. The intense time of prayer had sapped her energy. She prayed, "Lord, give me the strength I need to speak for you tonight."

It turned out to be a huge meeting in an amphitheater. After Evelyn was introduced, she stood and walked to the platform. As she did, she felt herself filled with strength and energy. She spoke that night with unusual freedom and power. The hearts of many were touched.

When Evelyn had finished her presentation and had prayed with the last person who sought her after her time of teaching, the leader of the conference told her, "A man in the audience tonight shared something unusual with me. He said that as you rose to speak, he saw two angels, one on either side of you. They supported you as you walked to your place on the platform and they remained with you as you talked, giving you strength throughout your time of teaching."

Evelyn had not seen the angels. She did know that on one of the most difficult days of her life she had sought to be faithful to her Lord and to forgive even when it was so difficult. Then the Lord blessed, as he always does, giving his strength and help when we need it most.

Forgiveness Takes Time

Evelyn Christenson is a mature Christian who walks daily with God. When the challenge came, she knew the biblical principles and began to apply them. Still, it took hours of intense soul searching and prayer for her to find the freedom of forgiveness. Even after this, there was the process of completing the work of forgiveness as she interacted with those members of her extended family in the days and weeks ahead. Evelyn had changed, but the others had not. Evelyn had committed herself to respond in a Christlike way, but the others had not. They would strike out in bitterness again and again. Evelyn had to forgive more times than one. She remembered how Jesus has taught us to forgive seventy times seven if needed.

Forgiveness does takes time. Often it takes more than a day or a week. Forgiveness is a process. It is like peeling an onion. When you peel back one layer, another layer awaits. Don't minimize the need or the process. Acknowledging your anger is like opening a wound. We need to take time to let it drain and heal.

When we have a problem, when we are hurt, we need to deal with it as soon as possible. Find the help of God. Begin the process outlined above and continue until peace and healing come.

FIFTEEN

꙳ᢙ꙳

Give the Gift
of Memories

A sweet old lady gives beautiful memories. We try to forget a grumpy old grouch.

We called her the Duchess. "I can't imagine why they call me that," Louise would always say. But everyone else knew. She looked and acted like a dowager.

She called in July to invite our family to dinner the first Saturday in December. It was not unusual for church members to invite their pastor and family to dinner, but it wasn't often the invitation came six months in advance. It was only later we understood the reason. Louise had made reservations at Riverside Inn, a charming restaurant in the country. She reserved early because she wanted to be certain she not only would get into the restaurant during the busy Christmas season but also that she would have the exact table she wanted.

The Duchess no longer drove, so when the first Saturday in December came, we picked her up in our car. She asked my husband and our two children to help her carry some mysterious boxes out to the car. When we arrived at the restaurant, she had them carry the boxes into the lobby but asked us to wait there until our table was ready. The owner of the restaurant greeted her by name. Obviously she had given him a thorough briefing as to what was to happen. He summoned a busboy to help her carry the boxes into the dining room while we waited in suspense. Finally the owner, acting as the maître d', escorted us to our table.

Louise stood there smiling, as if she were a duchess welcoming nobility into her castle. She had chosen the table by the beautiful fireplace. The mysterious boxes had been filled with antique Christmas decorations for the table. The Duchess had even brought her own tablecloth! Candles were burning in her silver candelabra. It looked like a page out of *House Beautiful*. What a glorious beginning to the Christmas season we had! When the evening closed, the Duchess made us promise to save the first Saturday night in December the following year. It was her Christmas gift to us. For ten years, as long as we were in the pastorate in Springfield, Missouri, we officially began our Christmas with Louise Stewart at Riverside Inn. It was always with the same ritual, at the same table, with the same family heirlooms decorating the table. Twenty years have passed. The Duchess now celebrates Christmas in heaven. But when the first Saturday in December comes, our family recalls with warmth and gratitude the gift of memories Louise gave to us.

The Duchess was not wealthy; she had to manage her widow's pension very carefully. She had to save to take our family of four to Riverside, but there was no doubt it was worth it to her. It gave her beautiful memories and something to anticipate through the year. She knew she was giving more than a dinner at a nice restaurant. She was giving the gift of memories. Our family and the Duchess were richer because of the gift. She will always be remembered by our family.

Family Gifts

Our goal has been to give the gift of memories to our children. Both my husband and I are Scandinavian, and during the Christmas season we keep many of the Swedish customs. On December 12 we celebrate Lucia Day, a day commemorating an early Christian martyr. Our daughter Sharon, from the time she was a little girl, would wear a white robe with a crimson sash and a crown of candles on her head. Early in the morning, accompanied by her brother Stephen as a star boy, she would bring saffron buns and coffee to her family at the break of day. Today our granddaughters, Aubrey and Angela, carry on the tradition.

On Christmas Eve our family has a smorgasbord with many traditional Swedish foods. The preparations for this Yule meal are a part of the fun. Today our children and grandchildren all work together in the kitchen, preparing the food, from Swedish meatballs to cookies. Christmas Day we have a birthday cake for Jesus. After reading about the birth of Jesus from the Bible, we all join in singing "Happy Birthday" to Jesus. For our children and grandchildren, the family rituals are awaited more eagerly than the opening of the Christmas presents. Most of the Christmas gifts of years gone by are forgotten but not the gift of memories.

One of the reasons I taught school for several years was that we might give memories of travel to our children. We would carefully plan trips we would take during vacation times that would include new experiences, fun, and learning as we journeyed together in our station wagon.

Tiny Treasures

Some of the best memories are small. It may be as simple as a smile or a touch. A friend gives a word of encouragement at the right time. A co-worker lends a helping hand when you are swamped with work. It may be an unexpected thank-you note or a little gift that says, "I care." Random acts of kindness are often long remembered.

Taking Risks

What memories stand out the most for people who have lived to be over ninety? Dr. Dale Purves from the Duke University Medical Center did a survey. He discovered the times they remembered most vividly were not their successes or failures. The periods that still lived in Technicolor for them were the times they took risks.

I'm not near the age of ninety yet, but I have found that even now the memories that stand out most clearly for me are the times involving a high degree of risk. The most memorable was one summer when our daughter and son were teenagers. We dared to allow strangers to live in our comfortable home in the Midwest while we went to live in a foreign country. My husband took the risk of having a man he had never met take over his position for the summer. If it didn't work out, Bill might not have had a job when he returned.

We exchanged pulpits with Jack Hair, a British pastor. For that summer, Bill served as pastor of the Florence Road Baptist Church in Brighton, England. He preached the sermons, taught the Bible studies, visited the sick and shut-ins, worked with the church board, performed funerals, and did all the ministries a parson does. The Reverend Jack Hair came from England and took Bill's place as the senior pastor of the University Heights Baptist Church in Springfield, Missouri. The Hairs moved into our house in Springfield, Missouri, and we lived in their church manse. We were not tourists. We soon discovered we had to learn to live like our British neighbors. Sometimes we risked our lives. We drove on the left side of the road (most of the time). Instead of shopping in the supermarket, we found ourselves going to the greengrocer, the butcher, and the baker. Sometimes we risked our pride. The things the British do without thinking caught us unprepared. We needed help in ordering fish and chips. We didn't know where to shop for things like pins. (They are to be found at the haberdashers'.)

We learned about the British system of socialized medicine when our son had an emergency appendectomy. Our daughter's favorite memory was quite different. Even as a teen, Sharon was a writer. When we went to Stratford-on-Avon, Timothy Dalton was playing the lead in Romeo and Juliet. Sharon arranged to interview him for *Seventeen* magazine. He met her after the performance at the Black Swan restaurant, which the locals called "The Dirty Duck." The interview lasted two and one-half hours. What a memory for a teenager!

We learned history by visiting castles and battlefields, museums and monuments. I took up brass rubbing, and while I would rub the brasses in a church (usually ones with angels) my husband would visit with the vicar. We learned to ride the British rail, explore London, and attend the theater.

"Don't feel hurt if no one invites you to their home," the British pastor had warned us. "The English have to know you for about ten years before they are likely to invite you into their homes." No one did invite us—for the first two weeks. Apparently they were sizing up the American family. After that, the invitations poured in. We were invited to more than thirty homes for tea or a meal. It was one of the greatest experiences of our lives. We were guests in the homes of the wealthy, the typical middle class, and the poor. There was never a lack of conversation. We discussed the British and American ways of life. We discovered many differences between British and American churches. We found ourselves having to examine many ideas that before we had always taken for granted. We ate foods that were new to us.

The usually reserved British shared their life experiences with us. Perhaps they felt comfortable doing this because they knew Bill is a pastor. More likely it was also the security that in a few weeks we would be thousands of miles and an ocean away.

Tea Time

Tea time is a treasured memory. I arranged for us to go for tea as often as possible. We had tea in famous restaurants, in village tearooms, in country farmhouses, and especially in the homes of parishioners. I observed tea etiquette and gathered recipes. Instead of buying many small souvenirs, I invested all I could afford in a set of Coalport china dishes with a beautiful band of cherubs that were made in England and never exported. Tea and the china were simply personal interests of mine at the time. I had no idea that years later I would be serving teas in my home. I never dreamed that one day British television would come to America to film my teas and that over half of the television sets in the United Kingdom would be watching as I served tea in my living room in the United States. My goal was just to give our family the gift of memories—of teatime in England.

Selecting the Gift

Sometimes shopping for a gift for someone is half the fun. Trying to find the right present for a person is a challenge. You may have to look in many places before you discover what you are looking for, but there is a feeling of satisfaction when the right choice is made.

Shopping for memories is similar, but it is also different in several respects. Some memories just happen. They are completely unplanned and spontaneous. They cost nothing. There is the magic moment when the full moon comes over the horizon and you are with the one you love. It may be just being there, silently, when someone you care about has a significant loss. It often is a word fitly spoken, sometimes a word of encouragement; other times, a sincere compliment given at the appropriate time.

Memories are also the result of planning. Sometimes it takes months of planning with many people involved. A wedding is an example of this. Holiday celebrations and vacations are other examples where everyone involved takes part in the anticipation and planning, and the preparations enhance the memories.

Other times, the person to whom the memory is given may be unaware of the arrangements being made. It may be a surprise birthday event or a retirement party. I have a friend who was delighted that one Friday his wife "kidnapped" him from his office at the end of the day. He was unaware that she had made reservations for a weekend get-away. She had arranged for a baby-sitter for the children (who were in on the surprise). She had his bag packed in the trunk of the car, and she didn't tell him what their destination was until they arrived.

There are untold opportunities to give the gift of memories. Gifts of memories are always appropriate. Give them to yourself and others. If you want to excel at this, you must look for the chance to say or do something that will be meaningful and appreciated. The person who looks for ways to bless is the one who is most often a blessing. Give the gift of memories as often as possible.

Choose Your Memories

"Every night I have trouble sleeping," Rose confided in me. "The memories of my past, especially the memories of my failures, just seem to sweep over me. I am filled with remorse over my wrong choices and my lost opportunities."

While this can be true at any age, for many it is a condition that intensifies with age. The joy of today is lost in regrets over yesterday. The poet captures the feeling common to us all.

> Across the fields of yesterday
> He sometimes comes to me.
> That little lad just in from play
> The lad I used to be.
> And yet he smiles so wistfully
> Once he has crept within.
> I wonder if he hoped to find
> The man I might have been.

Aren't there times we all wonder about the choices we have made and about the woman we might have become if only . . . ? I have had some dark nights of the soul. I have had memories and regrets come unbidden, especially during the night hours. What do we do when we are overcome with these unwelcome thoughts?

We can pray. We can ask the Lord for forgiveness. We can pray for those who have hurt us and for those who have been hurt by us. This is right and healthy, but not if we spend all night praying about all the hurts and mistakes of the past. Concentrating our prayers on the area of our regrets reinforces the pain and hurt. It is better to commit past situations to the Lord. Once given to him, we should move on. I have discovered a secret learned from the great Christians of the past. After praying for forgiveness and relinquishing the hurts of the past, claim God's unconditional love. Then move on and pray for someone else. Lift intercessory prayers for others that have no connection with the old wounds. Pray for the future with hope.

Then choose your memories. Yes, it is possible. We need not be passive and allow whatever may come to fill our minds. We can choose what we think about. "Whatever is true, whatever is noble, whatever is right, whatever is pure, whatever is lovely, whatever is admirable—if anything is excellent or praiseworthy—think about such things . . . And the God of peace will be with you" (Philippians 4:8–9). When a memory of a failure creeps into your mind, choose to think briefly about what you have gained from the experience. Almost always we gain through losing. Then choose to relive a pleasant memory. It may be one where you were loved and affirmed by another person. It may be of the time you overcame an obstacle. You could choose to remember a time of celebration.

I think of our friend Bertha. Her husband died a few months ago. This is the first Christmas in many years she will be without him. Her loss is real. Her sadness is genuine. "As Christmas comes, choose what you will think about," my husband pastor counseled her. "When you come to church for the Christmas services, don't dwell on the thought that Roy is no longer with you. Think about Christmas. Christmas means Christ the Lord was born. He came that we might have eternal life. God intends Christmas to bring hope and healing. Go to church to find the joy of the Lord. Remember the memories of the past and be thankful for them. Look forward to the future, that glorious future you will have when you will be reunited once again. Accept the Christmas gift of peace and joy God is offering you."

It's not easy, you may reply. Yes, it is sometimes difficult at the moment to choose the positive memories and the hopeful thoughts, but it is worth all the effort it takes to create this new habit. It makes a difference in how we make it through the night, the next day, and the rest of our lives.

Give the gift of memories to others. Choose to fill your mind with the warm, wonderful memories that will lift your spirit.

SIXTEEN

The Secret of Humor

A sweet old lady has a healthy sense of humor.
A grumpy old grouch finds life to be grim.

On one of the darkest days of the War Between the States, Abraham Lincoln assembled his cabinet. To their astonishment he began the cabinet meeting by reading from a book of humor by Artemus Ward. From time to time the president had to interrupt his reading because he was laughing so hard. The cabinet members were aghast. They sat silently through the reading. How could Mr. Lincoln take time for humor when the situation was so grim?

Finally President Lincoln closed the book and said, "Gentlemen, why don't you laugh? With the fearful strain that is on us, you need this as much as I."

Then Abraham Lincoln reached into his stovepipe hat and drew out what Stanton, one of the cabinet members, described as a slip of paper and read for the first time the Emancipation Proclamation.

Look on the Funny Side

Seeing the funny side, even when life is terrible, is a mark of maturity. The ability to find humor in ordinary life can make every day more enjoyable. We may not be able to choose the events of our lives, but we can choose our outlook. We can focus on the dark or look for the light. While staying in touch with reality, including the problems and difficulties of life, we can still look for those elements in each situation that will make us smile.

While this is important in every stage of life, it is even more important as each year passes. You have a choice in almost any situation you'll ever find yourself, and old age is no exception. You can be depressed and upset or optimistic and hopeful. It's all up to you. That's why keeping a sense of humor is so important as you get older, because most people seem to find more to feel gloomy about. It's as if the calendar gives them an excuse to feel sorry for themselves.

It is not easy to keep a sense of humor. Early in life many people around us try to persuade us that humor is out of place. Parents and teachers can often be heard saying, "Wipe that smile off your face." As we grow older, the people we work with are likely to admonish, "Get serious—this is no laughing matter." How often have you heard a bland, unhappy person interrupt a time of good, healthy laughter with the put-down, "When are you going to act your age?"

I was actually punished for laughing when I was a teenager. Our study hall teacher had left the room for a minute. During her absence, Smoky, who sat at the desk in front of me, left his seat to sharpen his pencil. Quickly a boy across the aisle slipped a tack on the empty seat. When Smoky returned to his chair, he sat squarely on the tack. Instantly he jumped to his feet, letting out the strangest yelp I had ever heard. It struck me so funny that I began to laugh. Of course, it was just then the teacher entered the room. "Marilynn," she ordered, "come to my desk immediately." She filled out a slip requiring me to remain after school for an hour of detention.

It seemed so unjust to me. I was innocent of placing the tack on my fellow student's seat. When I read the detention slip, I saw the teacher had not filled in the space giving the cause for my detention. I marched back to her desk to have her give an explanation for my punishment. She took her pen and in the blank that read *reason for detention,* the teacher wrote "hilarious laughter."

I spent my hour in the detention hall that day. I remember it as one of the best hours of my life. I was able to finish all my homework for the day, and one hour seemed a small price to pay for gales of hilarious laughter. It did not squelch my sense of humor.

After being told *not* to laugh so often through life, many people become cautious. In their effort to remain politically correct, they focus their attention on always being serious. They do not look for the humor in each situation. In time, they are so much out of practice, they may lose the ability to make themselves laugh even if they really want to.

Humor Has Benefits

If you develop your sense of humor, the first result is that life becomes more enjoyable. You will smile frequently and laugh more often. A funny insight can make the most boring chore tolerable. The situation that might humiliate you can be redeemed and turned into an enjoyable time. I learned this from my friend Olivia Barger.

"You'll never guess what happened to me," Olivia declared with a grin. "I have this new pair of gigantic earrings that I just love. I decided to show them off as I went shopping today. I was so pleased. Everywhere I went people kept looking at these beautiful, big earrings. In fact, I saw several people staring at them. When I got home, I told my husband, Bill, that wherever I went, people noticed my new earrings. 'Of course they did,' Bill replied. 'Olivia, you have your earrings on backward!'" And with that she burst into gales of laughter, thinking how ridiculous those big earrings must have looked. She was laughing at herself for imagining that people were admiring her new look when they were really thinking how ridiculous her earrings looked.

This was typical of the way Olivia faced life. She could have been embarrassed or let the incident devastate her. Instead, she chose to discover the humor in the ridiculous. Instead of crying, she had a good laugh. When she told the story to her friends, we all laughed, too. We didn't laugh at her. We admired Olivia for seeing the funny side of life and sharing it with us. Years later when I see a pair of large earrings, a smile creeps across my face as I remember Olivia's sparkling eyes and contagious laughter as she told the story.

Humor Attracts Friends

Humorless people are dull and cheerless. People avoid them. We are attracted to a person who smiles and enjoys life and laughter. Children are hesitant about adults who are always solemn, but they are drawn to those who are cheerful. Friends who are fun to be with have a gentle wit and inject a quiet element of mirth into their conversations. It is important to learn the proper balance. The jokester who has a quip about everything can be more tiresome than the unsmiling bore, but the person with a sparkling sense of humor will win friends by the score.

Humor Can Be a Lifesaver

The atmosphere grows tense. Humor can relieve it. Someone is certain the sky is falling. Humor can place things in perspective. People become critical, perhaps even catty. The spice of a gentle wit can often diffuse the situation and move the conversation to a more pleasant level.

Steve Allen, the famous comic, grew up in a rough neighborhood. He says, "Being funny was sometimes necessary for survival. Making the bullies on the corner laugh was the best way to avoid being beaten up."

My husband, Bill, found that to be true early in our married life. We were living on the south side of Chicago while Bill was finishing graduate school. One night, while I was baking, I used the last of the milk in the refrigerator. "Bill," I called. "We're out of milk. We won't have any for breakfast in the morning."

"I can solve that problem easily," my husband replied. "There's a new machine they've just put on Halsted Street that dispenses half gallon cartons of milk day or night. I'll take a pocketful of change and be back with your milk in no time."

It was after ten o'clock in the evening when Bill left the house. He drove five blocks to the corner where the milk machine stood. Bill read the directions (he always reads directions), placed the proper coins in the machine, and a half-gallon carton of milk slid into an opening below. Bill took the milk and turned to return to his car. To his surprise, he found a dozen tough-looking street kids standing in a circle around his car. *This looks like trouble,* Bill thought. Quickly he considered his options. None of them looked good. Silently he prayed for protection and wisdom. *Don't panic,* an inner voice seemed to say. *Talk to them.*

Bill walked toward his car. As he approached, the gang stood shoulder to shoulder, creating a barrier between him and his automobile. The sneers on their faces and the defiance in their body language seemed meant to taunt him.

"Hello," Bill said, trying to sound as unconcerned as possible as he walked toward the door on the driver's side of the car. He was praying they would move aside and let him in.

"Hello, yourself," a muscular young man in black leather sneered back. The dozen street kids did not move. Bill was now standing face-to-face with their leader.

"How's Tom?" the leader asked.

Bill had no idea what to make of the question. *Tom? What Tom?* he thought. *I'm certain I don't know anyone these kids know.* But the question called for a response. Bill stalled for time. "I haven't seen Tom for days," he replied.

"How's Julie?" the leader persisted.

Obviously they were playing some kind of game. The street gang knew the rules. Bill did not, but he kept his cool as he answered, "Julie? If Julie has been around, I haven't seen her."

The leader looked Bill squarely in the eye and asked, "How's Chuck?"

The thought came to Bill, *This gang is out to have a good time. Right now they are having it at my expense, making me uncomfortable because I don't know what is going to happen next. Suppose I give an answer they don't expect. Suppose I take them by surprise, and we all have fun doing it?*

"Chuck?" Bill replied. "Haven't you heard? Chuck is a street car conductor!"

"A street car conductor?" the whole gang repeated, almost in unison. It was the last thing they had expected to hear. Since my husband and I are both Scandinavian, Bill began to talk in a heavy Scandinavian accent. Another surprise but one calculated to signal that this was going to be fun.

"Yah, them street car conductors are pretty smart fellows. Why, the other day I got on a street car and sat down. I thought the seat next to me was empty, but to my surprise there was a small pocketbook lying there. *I wonder who lost it?* I thought to myself. 'Not to worry,' I told myself. 'It was lost on the street car and it is the street car conductor's problem to find the owner. Them street car conductors are pretty smart fellows.'

"Well, we bumped along for a minute, then the street car jerked to a stop. The street car conductor looked around and called out, 'Madison!' And would you believe it, just as big as life, Mr. Madison got up and got off that street car.

"We bumped along for another couple of blocks and the street car stopped again. 'Washington,' the street car conductor called out. And would you believe it, Mr. Washington got up and got off the street car. That street car conductor knew everyone on his street car and where they were to get off. Them street car conductors are pretty smart fellows.

"We bumped along a little farther. Then suddenly the street car stopped. The conductor looked around, not so certain this time. 'Jackson!' he called out. Now my name is Jackson, so I got up and got off that street car. I wondered why he put me off there. I had never been on the street corner before, but I thought them street car conductors are pretty smart fellows. There must be a reason.

"Then I remembered the pocketbook. I wondered if there was any money in it. I opened it and began to count, 'One dollar, two dollars, three dollars.' Just then a man came up to me. I had never seen him before in my life, honest. He said to me, 'Excuse me, but I am looking for Jackson.'

"'This is Jackson,' I said proudly.

"'I am looking for sixteen fifty-three,' the stranger said.

"'Mister, here is your money,' I said and I gave him his pocketbook. Them street car conductors are pretty smart fellows."

The story left the street gang in stitches. "Mister, who are you, anyway?" one of them called out.

"I'm the youth pastor at the Foster Park Baptist Church," Bill replied. "Here, take my card and come see me at my place sometime."

"Maybe," the leader replied.

Now no one was standing between Bill and his car, so he opened the door, waved to the gang, and drove off. The next day he discovered that gang had stolen a policeman's nightstick and roughed him up considerably. Humor can change the situation you find yourself in and can even save your life.

Humor Relieves Stress

Dr. Stephen Allen, Jr., Steve's eldest son, is a physician in Elmira, New York. He regularly gives workshops on stress reduction. Humor is an important tool in combating stress, he reports. He talks about *creative silliness*. "Putting playfulness into every day makes you work more creatively, no matter what your job," Steve, Jr. teaches. "I tell people to ask themselves: 'Do I know where my silliness is today?' If they haven't had it out for a while, they should get silly immediately."

Humor Can Bring Physical Benefits

At the age of fifty, Norman Cousins, the noted critic and *Saturday Review* editor, was stricken with a crippling form of spinal arthritis. He was told there was no known cure for the disease, and his doctor advised him to get his affairs in order. Cousins fell into a deep depression. The more depressed he became, the worse his disease got and the more intense his pain became.

Cousins decided to fight back. The doctors were doing what could be done for his medical condition, so Cousins decided to fight his depression. His friend Alan Funt sent him copies of the *Candid Camera* TV show, and Cousins sent out for some old Marx Brothers movies. Soon he was laughing so hard his sides ached and his eyes watered. "I made the joyous discovery that ten minutes of genuine belly laughter had an anesthetic effect and would give me at least two hours of pain-free sleep," he would later write in his best-selling book, *Anatomy of an Illness.* "The more I laughed, the better I got." Soon he was able to check into a nearby hotel where he could "laugh twice as hard at half the price."

Cousins did not die but went on to study the effects of positive emotions on healing. He became a regular lecturer at the medical school at the University of California at Los Angeles. "You can't 'ha-ha' your way out of a serious illness," he advised. "Laughter is no substitute for competent medical attention, and humor should be a part of an overall treatment plan. I always emphasize that I never abandoned what my doctors prescribed." In his lectures to medical students, Cousins cited evidence that deep hearty laughter can improve lung respiration, oxygenate the blood, and promote the body's production of endorphins, the natural pain killers that enhance our general sense of well-being.

Laugh at Yourself, Not at Others

While it is true that we can find humor in all of life, not everything is a laughing matter. There are some guidelines to using humor. The first is, Laugh at yourself. Don't make another person the butt of your jokes.

A favorite story spread like wildfire through the retirement community where my husband Bill was the administrator illustrates this point. It was reported to have been in our local newspaper.

At that time a television commercial that was shown repeatedly, advertised a device that was worn like a necklace.

If a person needed help, she could press a button and immediately be connected to 911 and its emergency services. One commercial showed a white-haired woman who had fallen. She pressed the button, and when the 911 operator responded, she was heard saying, "Help. I've fallen and I can't get up."

An elderly woman in our city who lived alone had purchased the new device. One morning she pulled her garbage can out to the curb for pick up. The small can was only half full, but it took all the energy the little old lady had to get it to the curb. She needed to rest but there was no place to sit except on the garbage can. But when she sat on the can, she fell in and was unable to get out. She pressed her emergency button and the 911 operator responded. "Help! I've fallen and I can't get up," the elderly lady said.

"Where are you?" the operator asked.

"I'm in the garbage can in front of my house," came the reply. Then she gave her address.

When the residents of the retirement home told the story, they would add, "Can you imagine how embarrassing it would be sitting in the garbage can waiting for the paramedics to come?"

They could imagine. The incident was close to their life situation. Most of them were concerned about their health and had considered buying such an emergency signaling device. Getting stuck in a garbage can was a ridiculous twist to the commercial they had all seen. It's the kind of thing that could have happened to them. That's what made it funny.

It would have been even funnier to hear the little old lady tell the story on herself. Did she find the incident to be funny? Possibly not. She could have been embarrassed. She might have been mortified when the story came out in the paper. If she was present and someone said, "Let me tell you what happened to her," and recounted how she was stuck in the garbage can, it would be cruel and humiliating. The safest rule is laugh at yourself, not at another person.

This is especially true with racial or ethnic humor. If you tell a story about the foibles of your own group, it can be funny. If you tell the same story that makes fun of some other group, especially if those persons are present, it is insensitive. Stories that point out idiosyncrasies of other people can be demeaning.

Keep a Healthy Balance

Humor is like salt. A sprinkling of it can add zest. Too much can spoil everything. People will avoid the person who has a quip about everything. There is a time to laugh and a time to be serious. Often the deepest and most genuine laughter comes during serious times. When appropriate, it is natural, never forced. It has its place but does not supplant the seriousness of the occasion.

Don't overdo humor. Resist the temptation to "top" every funny story someone else tells. A spirit of competition can be a way of putting another person down, and that is not funny. A person with a good sense of humor enjoys the humor of others. It is not necessary to be the life of every party.

Be Appropriate

I was working on a project recently with a group of women. One young gal was so intent on being funny that in a few minutes she was a source of irritation to everyone. It wasn't that her jokes, judged individually, were so bad. We had so much to do and we were behind schedule, and her jokes were seen as a distraction. She missed one important clue. No one was laughing. That should always be a signal that humor is not appropriate.

Some subjects are not appropriate for most situations, even if they strike some as being funny. Talking dirty or telling stories about sex or toilet functions are best left unsaid. Although they may appeal to some, they are likely to be offensive to others.

Enjoy! Enjoy!

Studies show that almost everyone believes he or she has a fine sense of humor. In fact, most people think they have a better sense of humor than other people. Are you one of these?

If so, don't let this keep you from cultivating and developing the gift you have. Since a sense of humor is important, it is a legitimate quest to expand and refine it. Be open to seeing the funny side of life, especially your own life. Smile often. Don't hesitate to laugh out loud. Be increasingly joyful.

SEVENTEEN

Develop a Vital Faith

*A sweet old lady develops a vital faith. A
grumpy old grouch ignores God.*

wo children came into their grandmother's room and
found her reading the Bible. "What is she doing?" the
younger one asked.

"I think she's cramming for finals," the older girl explained.

A vital faith is more than cramming for finals. In his book,
Learn to Grow Old, Dr. Paul Tournier writes, "The happiest and
most content old people are those with a vital faith. It not only
helps them face dying but helps them live day by day."

Studies have shown that the happiest young people and
the happiest middle-aged people are those with a strong and
vibrant faith. It doesn't matter who does the study. Those done
by *Redbook* or *Cosmopolitan* magazines show results similar to
those done by church groups or university-based researchers.
Regardless of age, income level, or social standing, the happiest people are those who say that their trust in God is very
important and that they make a genuine effort to practice their
beliefs. The famous psychoanalyst, Carl Gustav Jung, reported
that in all his practice he had never had a single client come
to full maturity and satisfaction in life who did not develop a
strong personal faith.

The more a person lives by faith, the more faith grows. The
more faith grows, the happier one becomes. The happiest older

ladies are the ones who have been practicing Christians the longest. "Sweeter as the years go by" aptly describes both the woman of faith and the object of her faith.

Whatever your age, the wisest thing you can do is to develop a vital faith. It is the single most important aspect of your life. It will enhance your relationships with others. It will give you stability when life comes tumbling in around you and will add joy and meaning to your successes in life.

Begin with Commitment

I accepted Christ when I was young. I was raised in a Christian home, and I found it as natural to believe that my heavenly Father loved me as much as my earthly father did. When I was in grade school, a child evangelism teacher asked if I would like to give my life to Jesus. I said, "Yes," and together we prayed a prayer of commitment. Although I was young, I was sincere, and this decision was genuine. I gave as much of my life to God as I knew how.

As I grew into my teen years, I discovered new areas of my life that needed to be given over to God's control. As I made my passages through adulthood, I found repeatedly that new stages in growth called for fresh commitments. As a child, I had no idea of the challenges, pressures, and temptations that would come later in life. At each point in my development all I could do was to give myself to God as much as I knew how, but it all began with that first decision to follow Christ.

I have always been interested in various religious experiences people have. My friend Esther's experience was completely different from mine. Esther had been raised in a home that was hostile to any religion. She had only been inside a church to attend weddings and funerals. She made no secret of her antagonism toward organized religion. "If it feels good, do it," had been her motto through college. At twenty-six she had done it all, but instead of finding fulfillment, she was disillusioned. She not only hit bottom; she crashed. Feeling all alone, her thoughts turned to Mary, a sorority sister who was living in the same town. Esther had not seen Mary for years, but she remembered that she had always been the life of the party. In desperation she called and asked Mary to meet her at an all-night coffee shop. An hour later they were together.

Esther was surprised to hear herself saying, "I can't go on. I'm miserable and tormented by guilt over the way I have been living. Life has no meaning. I've tried everything, but I'm just empty, completely empty inside."

"You've tried everything else," Mary replied. "Don't you think it's time to try Jesus? I did, and I found he filled that vacuum I had always been feeling."

The two talked for three hours. Before they left, Mary led Esther in a simple prayer, asking God for forgiveness and opening her life to Christ. That decision changed her life forever.

The Woman Who Had Everything

How different from another friend. Gloria was a college graduate, happily married with an all-American family. She was a leader in her profession. Her friends recognized that she was a person of maturity and personal strength. Her life had enough meaning, and Gloria had enough self-worth to feel content and basically happy. Her attitude toward the church was, "Thanks, but no thanks. If you find help there, that's great for you, but I can get along without it."

Gloria met Marcia at the symphony guild. They discovered they belonged to the same athletic club and had much in common. Gloria and Marcia began to do lunch together every week or ten days. Soon a fast friendship had formed. They talked about their families, their professions, and their community interests. Marcia often spoke about her faith in Christ as well. One day Gloria inquired, "You are happy, capable, and well-adjusted. Why is religion important to you? Is it that you were raised in the church?"

"No," Marcia replied. "I didn't become a Christian until I was about thirty. I was secure and content. and really enjoying life and its blessings. Then Jesus showed me I could find even greater joy. It began when I recognized that all I had, including my talents and abilities, were gifts from God. When that dawned on me, I prayed my first real prayer. It was something like this: 'God, I'm so blessed, but I've never stopped to really thank you. I can't take the credit for who and what I am. It was you who made me this way. You must really love me. Now help me to love you back like I should.' When I opened my life to Christ that way, other things began to come into focus."

"Like what?" Gloria asked. "Do you have some deep, dark secrets in your past you haven't told me?"

"Oh, no," Marcia laughed. "I was somewhat rebellious in my teen years, but I have never done anything people would consider to be terrible or a big sin. I haven't had an affair or embezzled money or any of those things. It's just that I was concerned with my own happiness and preoccupied with my own problems."

"That pretty well describes me," Gloria responded. "Is that so bad?"

"I didn't think so then," Marcia explained. "Now I see I was really missing the main thing in life—God! I needed to ask his forgiveness for ignoring him for so long, for taking him for granted, for doing my own thing without any concern for what his plan was. For me, getting right with God was opening up to him so that he was the new center of my life. In losing my life for him and using my blessings for others and his work, I found my true life."

"That makes sense," Gloria responded. "I'm not ready to do it myself, at least not yet. Give me some time to think about it."

A week later Gloria said, "I've been doing a lot of soul-searching, and I'm ready." The two women prayed together. It was a simple and genuine prayer. Gloria did not hear angels sing, nor did she have a deep emotional experience. "I did commit myself to Christ," she explains, "and I know he accepted me. I know I am forgiven and I have a new orientation in life. It's been a new birth for me. One that will last for eternity."

The Next Step

It all begins with commitment, but several elements come into play in the adventure of faith. Once the decision has been made for Christ, it is vital to learn more about him. Fortunately, this is easy. God has revealed himself through Jesus Christ, and we have the record of him in the Bible. When one reads and rereads the Gospels, we learn much of who Jesus is. As we go through the Bible, we discover what is important to God, what he is like, what he values, and what is unimportant to him.

Fortunately, we are not the only ones making this search. Networking with other Christians is so helpful. Their insights and experiences can help us understand more fully who Jesus is and what he is doing in the world today. We can learn from their struggles and triumphs. Some of this will be found in Sunday worship and church Bible studies. We discover far more if we become a part of a small group where Christians pray for each other and are able to talk about their Christian pilgrimage. Stick close to God's people.

> We share our mutual woes,
> Our mutual burdens bear;
> And often for each other flows
> The sympathizing tear.
>
> John Fawcett

Getting to Know Him

But ours is not a search for the facts about Jesus alone. While doctrine may be important, our chief concern is that we may know Jesus Christ himself. What we learn about him helps us to know him more fully. One picture of this relationship that is found in the Bible is that of friendship. David was "a friend of God." That relationship was more important than what David did, including being king and writing the Psalms. Our goal is to be a friend of God. God does not have favorites, but he does have intimates, and he encourages each one of us to enter into this relationship.

Keep Talking

Everyone agrees that the key to any relationship is communication. It is the same with our relationship with God. If we would develop a vital faith we must talk to him often. We call this prayer. Set aside a time in your day as your appointment with God.

I like to keep a prayer basket. This helpful suggestion came from my friend Emilie Barnes. My basket has:

1. *A Bible.* I begin my time with God listening to what he has to say to me in his Word.
2. *A devotional book.* How precious to gain insights about our Lord from other Christians. I often find they have discovered truths I would never have thought of myself.
3. *My prayer notebook.* Keeping a written prayer list helps me to remember those I pray for. It also reminds me of the prayers that have been answered.
4. *Some pretty silk flowers* to remind me of the beauty of Jesus. They move me to pray, "Let the beauty of Jesus be seen in me."
5. *A small box of tissues* for the times I cry in joy or pain. I have a box with an angel design that I keep refilling. It reminds me that the angels join in my praise and adoration.
6. *A pen and a pad of paper.* Often during my quiet time, thoughts come crashing into my mind, usually of things I need to do. I find that when I write them down I can dismiss them from my mind and turn my thoughts again to God.
7. *A small supply of notecards and stamps.* Usually I write just a brief note to encourage someone or let him or her know I am praying for them.

Emilie Barnes writes, "Seeing my basket waiting for me is a wonderful invitation to times of prayer and a reminder when I haven't taken the time to pray." I find a basket to be helpful. It keeps all the things for my quiet time in one place, and if it is a beautiful day, I can take it outside with me.

Practicing the Presence

My Swedish mother used to quote a Scandinavian proverb. Translated it said, "Company and fish begin to smell after three days." It is often true that friends and relatives become difficult to live with when they are always there. Not so with Jesus! He offers his unconditional love. He always has our best interests at heart. He sees not only what we do but he also understands our motives as well. He is always calling us to be our best. At times I confess I am uncomfortable to realize that God is with me. That comes when I make choices that are selfish or sinful. Usually I block the heavenly presence from my earthly thoughts, but that does not change the reality that God is always there. He is especially active during those times, preparing a way for me to escape temptation or convicting me of my sin and calling me back to love and closeness once again.

A daily quiet time is so important, but it should be only a small part of our prayer life. We need to include the Lord in all we do and talk with him as we go through our day. Carl Jung had these words over the entryway to his home, "Whether invoked or not, God will be present." He is there, and it is such a blessing to go through the day talking with him.

This kind of prayer is different from the quiet time. It may be anything but! I remember times as my children were growing up that the kitchen was noisy and I was busy with all kinds of frantic activity. At that period of my life this was a favorite poem:

> Lord of all pots and pans and things,
> Since I've no time to be
> A saint by doing lovely things
> Or waiting late with Thee
> Or watching in the moonlight
> And storming heaven's gates,
> Make me a saint by getting meals
> And washing up the plates.

Cecily R. Hallack

The most ordinary tasks of a homemaker are pleasing to God and can be done as a service to him. What is even better is that the most boring, routine chores become far more tolerable if we talk with God while we are doing them. I have found it doesn't matter a great deal what I have to do if I can be with someone I love while I am doing it. Sometimes that person is my spouse; always it is Jesus Christ. For this kind of prayer there are often no words, just living in his presence.

The Cauldron of the Classroom

I recall the day I was asked to teach sixth grade in one of our local schools. I have taught elementary through high school, but sixth grade has always been my favorite grade to teach. I had not planned to teach that year, but the principal was urging me to reconsider. "Why are you needing a teacher now?" I asked. "There have already been ten weeks of classes."

"This is a difficult class," the principal admitted. "The first teacher left because she was unable to handle the classroom. Since then, we have had others try, but they only lasted a few days. Looking over your file, we think you are just what this class needs. Please come and help these children."

I did. I had prayed about it and had talked with my family. We all felt it was what I should do. The first day I wondered why I had accepted. The children were very intelligent. Most of their parents were college graduates. They seemed determined to run off every teacher. They had developed their skills in being a difficult class, practicing on the teachers before me. In the public school classroom, I knew my prayers would have to be silent, and I prayed as often as I could. They tended to be short SOS prayers as I found I needed to keep on top of the students every minute.

"Lord, I can't do this myself," I prayed. "You've got to help me!" I had a sense of his presence with me that gave me a feeling of stability. The students thought the odds were on their side. After all, it was thirty kids against one teacher. I saw it differently. It was not teacher against students; I was for them. But

I knew it was not up to me. The Lord was there working through me to help this class have the order and discipline necessary to learn. I don't think I smiled for a week, but I prayed that those sixth graders would sense that I genuinely cared about them and was doing what was in their best interest. That became one of my favorite classes. The district named me one of their merit teachers. I saw it as God's gracious answer to my fervent prayers.

Obedience: Keeping Priorities Straight

Too often we think of faith as finding a way for God to help us. It is true. He does help us, but that is not the central reason for our commitment. A vital faith means that we have chosen to follow Jesus, not that he will follow us around looking for ways to help us. He is the Lord of the universe. He is in charge.

That means I am committed to do his will. If I see my prayer basket and realize I have skipped my quiet time, I don't make excuses. I pick up my basket and keep my appointment with him. When I read in the Bible that we are to help the needy, I look for ways that I can help. When the Spirit calls to mind the command, "Love your enemies" I know there is no place for argument. It may be very, very hard, but it is my task to obey. If it takes time, I need to open my heart to him so he can be a part of the process. When life becomes busy and I am snowed under, I need to remember to keep my priorities straight. My first priority is Jesus Christ!

EIGHTEEN

The Golden Key: Contentment

A sweet old lady is content. A grumpy old grouch has many complaints.

The majority of us go through life unnoticed by the media. Most days are filled with ordinary activities. Even when our daily routine is interrupted by some event we consider special, few people close to us are very impressed. The editor of our local paper will rarely consider our achievement to be news and, if it does make our hometown newspaper, it is most unlikely to receive national coverage. We will never be the center of a ticker-tape parade. No one will erect a monument in our honor.

The infomercials on television try to persuade us that being ordinary is bad. The conventional wisdom is that anyone can become whatever she would like to be if only she would try hard enough. For those of us who live quiet, unheralded lives, it is easy for our self-image to suffer. We realize that in many ways we are average; we equate being average with being mediocre and consider settling for mediocrity to be a cop-out. How sad!

Personal success is found when we do what we can with the ability and opportunities we have and rejoice in what we have accomplished. Happiness is found in using our God-given potential and not coveting the ability, the fame, or the wealth that others may have. Success in life does not depend on recognition by the multitudes; rather, it is being faithful in doing what we can with what we have in the situation we find ourselves.

A woman can be a successful parent even if she has not been named the mother of the year. For every Julia Child, thousands of cooks have succeeded because they have kept their families fed, sometimes under the most trying circumstances. One person may achieve by authoring a best-selling book; another by writing encouraging letters to friends and family. One woman is important because she has climbed the corporate ladder into top management; another may be equally important because she manages a home.

Most things in life are done by quite ordinary people. The greatest amount of happiness in the world comes from the actions of countless individuals who go unnoticed by the superstars. Needy and hurting people are waiting for someone like us to come along. Many need our compassion, our encouragement, and our unique talents. When we share what we have to give, others will live a happier life. We give out of love. Love is the greatest force in the world.

Leo Buscaglia wrote, "Too often we underestimate the power of a touch, a smile, a kind word, an honest compliment, or the smallest act of caring, all of which have the potential to turn a life around. It's overwhelming to consider the continuous opportunities there are to make our love felt."

Lee Webber, my husband's oldest brother, was always a high achiever. He was president of his senior class in college. As a pastor, he led a church that grew into one of the largest congregations in the Northeast. He was a radio preacher whose messages were broadcast to much of the world. A hard worker, he went without vacations. "The Devil never takes a vacation," he would sometimes say. He was admired by many for his hard work, accomplishments, and dedication to God. He was known for his ability to make spiritual truths understandable and apply biblical truths in a practical way, but he made his greatest spiritual discovery in a most unusual way. Here is his first-person account.

Lee's Story

I have discovered a golden key to life. If I just tell you what it is, perhaps you will not understand. So let me tell you how I found it. It may help you when you are in the midst of troubles.

I was in the hospital after a heart attack. Being in the hospital is never easy under any circumstances. First, they take away your clothes, and part of your personality is wrapped up in what you wear. This is not only how the world sees you but also how you perceive yourself. Once you put on a hospital gown, something happens to you. There is a feeling of being under the control of others. You are told what to do and when to do it. Of course, this is necessary, but it certainly changes one's personal routine.

Perhaps the most difficult thing for me to face was the uncertainty of the future. I found this to be far greater than any pain or inconvenience my malady might make me suffer. I found myself asking, "What will happen to me now?" It was a question I could not answer.

After a series of tests, the doctor came to see me late one night and said, "It's open-heart surgery for you."

Thousands of people have heard those words, and I suppose no one welcomed them. But this was the second time I had heard these words, and I think they were more difficult to face the second time around. For five years I had coped with the problems and hoped for the future; now I was back to square one. I had to go home and wait my turn for surgery. This gave me time to think and evaluate my position.

I am a man of faith, and I am surrounded by people of faith. In my church one Sunday morning hundreds of people gathered around me and prayed that the God who can do all things would be pleased to reach down his hand and heal me so I would not have to face open-heart surgery again. *What a great solution to my problem,* I thought. *What a good testimony this would be to the healing power of God.*

But it was not to be. Hundreds prayed in faith and expected a miracle, but it never came. I thought about this over and over. I sought for an answer.

I knew God had not forsaken me, and I knew he would see me through. This was the help I needed to face my problems. But I saw my wife standing alongside me, and it seemed to be harder on her than it was on me. I thought I ought to put some things down on paper, and gradually some lines began to form in my mind. I wrote these out, and before leaving for the hospital, I put this page in a place where she would find it when she came home. These were the lines I wrote:

> I came to the swift, raging river,
> And the roar held the echo of fear.
> "Oh, Lord, give me wings to fly over,
> If you are, as you promised, quite near."
>
> But He said, "Trust the grace I am giving,
> All-pervasive, sufficient for you.
> Take my hand. We will face this together,
> But my plan is—not over, but through."

I suppose everyone hopes that after paying a tremendous price everything will work out and things will be all right. I was no exception. But it was not to be so. Even before I left the hospital, it was obvious the operation had been less than successful. I was going to have to make many difficult adjustments.

I came home from the hospital under heavy medication, sick, and weak. My whole future was a question mark.

I was physically and emotionally drained. I found myself at the lowest point in my life. I could hardly lift my head from the pillow, and the hours seemed to drag by. Then I remembered what a help it had been to have the assurance that the Lord would see me through and to put my thoughts down on paper. I thought I should do the same with the situation I was now facing. Too weak to sit up, I wrote the following words:

> At times it is easy to trust Him,
> And the promises shine like a light.
> "Oh, Lord, I am willing to trust You,
> But I don't want to walk in the night."
>
> But He said, "You can trust me whatever;
> When courage and strength are all gone;
> When nothing seems right or seems easy,
> When all you can do is hang on."

I did hang on, and after a while, I went back to preaching on Sunday mornings. What a joy this was! Since I was so limited in my physical activities, I had ample time for prayer and study, which is rare for a preacher. I did not have the energy to go to church to handle the hundreds of tasks that fall to the pastor, so I spent my time in the study at home. On Sunday mornings I would pour out my heart to the congregation while sitting on a high stool. I thought, *Well, Lord, if this is all I can do, I will do this with joy and pray that I can be a blessing to the people of my church.*

But each week it became more difficult. Every Sunday took a higher toll. I could see that even this limited activity was more than my strength would allow. But I could not give up the ministry! I had not reached retirement age. I had been a pastor for forty years and had preached nearly every Sunday for all that time. What would happen to me if I could not preach? I honestly did not know. I realized I would not survive if I continued. But could I give it up? Could I live without it?

I had no choice. I had to learn to trust the Lord in this most difficult decision. It was much harder than deciding on surgery. This was my ministry, my life. I had planned to continue serving the Lord as long as I had any breath in my body. I never intended to sit in a chair and watch the world go by. "Why should this happen to me?" I asked. "I have so much more to give, and I can share God's truth better than when I was in my youth." As I was thinking these things, I began to recall some lines written by the great poet Milton. I had memorized his sonnet on his blindness:

When I consider how my light is spent...

He was lamenting the same thing. I realized that out of all the poetry Milton wrote no line is so well-remembered as the last line of that sonnet:

They also serve who only stand and wait.

I was not the first to face this problem. Then I remembered that the apostle Paul had prayed the same prayer I was praying. He prayed concerning his thorn in the flesh. He told the Lord he had a great desire to serve and could serve so much better if only the Lord would remove this hindrance. That was my prayer! But the Lord said to Paul, "My grace is sufficient for you, for my strength is made perfect in weakness."

That is easy to say, but is it true? Is his grace sufficient? If it is, then my problem was a spiritual problem and needed a spiritual solution. I spent long periods of time with my Bible and the hymnbook. I found that many hymns were saying the things my heart was trying to say—the Lord would lead me; the Lord would see me through. As I meditated on the Twenty-third Psalm I found comfort rephrasing it in my own words:

Like a shepherd, Jesus leads me.
 I am safe within His care.
Waters cool I see before me,
 And the green grass everywhere.
Oh, my soul, refreshed you shall be
 And His name forever bless.
See my way is straight before me,
 And my paths are righteousness.

There are valleys, there are shadows,
 But with Him I never fear.

At His table there are no foes,
  Even though they gather near.
Oil anoints me, blessings throng me,
  Goodness, mercy guard my way.
In His house my dwelling shall be,
  When I end life's little day.

I had no choice. I could preach no longer. My health and strength grew weaker almost daily. I could carry no responsibilities. I could do no ministry, although this had been my life. I realized that if I rebelled against my condition, that kind of inner turmoil would literally kill me. I had to come to terms with myself and with my situation. I gathered my thoughts and put this down on paper:

We may quickly be discouraged by our faults and by
  our sin;
We may look upon this world with jaundiced eye.
We may moan about our troubles, we may turn our
  thoughts within;
And in pity, we may sit alone and cry.

But I do not choose to live life in this sad and
  gloomy way;
I can rest upon the Lord and see the sun.
Though the clouds may cast a shadow, there is hope
  beyond today;
There's the promise I will hear His "Child, well
  done."

So I may not have the best of all conditions in this
  life.
There are many things I wish were not this way.
But I'll do the best I can, and I will rise above the
  strife,
And I'll fill the air with singing every day.

I was beginning to see that in God's plan, there must be a key to dealing with this problem. I could still read the Bible, and I was working my way slowly through the book of Exodus. I read about Moses and how he was forced to flee from Egypt. He found himself far from the court of Pharaoh without authority, without responsibility, alone with the sheep of his father-in-law Jethro. As I read, Exodus 2:21 leaped off the page and into my heart. The Scripture says, "He was content to dwell with the man." Hidden in that verse was the key—"He *was content*." For forty years he was on the sidelines, in the middle of nowhere, on the back side of the desert, and he was content.

Could it be this was the word from God for which I was searching? Was the golden key as simple as that—to be content? As I thought about this, I remembered the old hymn:

> My Lord, how full of sweet content
> I pass my years of banishment!
> Where're I dwell, I dwell with Thee,
> In heav'n, in earth, or in the sea.

I had sung that hymn many times and had memorized its verses. Certainly it was true; contentment is possible in any circumstance.

Then I remembered how the apostle Paul wrote, "I have learned to be content whatever the circumstances" (Philippians 4:11). The dawn came up like thunder. The key to life is indeed contentment and contentment is something that must be learned. Paul had seen all his great missionary activity come to a halt. He was confined in prison, expecting execution. Could a person be content under these circumstances? Yes! Paul said, "I have learned to be content."

I remembered another verse, Hebrews 13:5. "Be content with what you have, because God has said, 'Never will I never leave you; never will I forsake you.'" I could see it clearly now. Our problems arise when we brood on the things we have lost—lost abilities, lost ministries, lost health, lost possessions, lost loved ones. While we mourn these things, the golden key of contentment slips through our fingers. Ruminating on our losses keeps us from experiencing the loving, healing, joyful presence of God, who said, "I will never leave you; never will I forsake you."

I realized that if my heart was set on that which was not possible for me, I was doomed to disappointment. This would never be the will of God for me. Could I learn to be content without an active ministry? Yes! Could I learn to be content with very severe physical limitations? Yes!

I recall that in the past I had preached on 1 Timothy 6:6, "But godliness with contentment is great gain." My emphasis had been on the importance of godliness. Now I began to see it in a different light. The verse is telling us that godliness by itself is not enough. You can be a godly person and live a frustrated, unhappy, unfulfilled life. There is a better way. It is the willingness to take one day at a time from the good hand of God and be content with what he gives, rejoicing in what we have and being aware of his presence.

Fifteen Years Later

Fifteen years have passed since Lee's second open-heart surgery. Today he moves with effort from his bed to his wheelchair. Even our telephone calls must be brief now because his energy is so limited. But when we talk, one thing comes through. Lee is content.

We can choose what we will think about. If we continually remember our losses or focus on what we do not have but wish we had, the result will always be unhappiness. If we count our blessings, if we approach each day with gratitude, there will be joy. We can do more. We can open our lives to the presence of God. In his presence is fullness of joy. As we learn to live life in God's presence, delighting in his will, we will discover that he is more important than our circumstances. We can learn to be content. That is the golden key.

NINETEEN
❦

Old Is Not a
Four-Letter Word

*All of life is cherished by a sweet old lady. A
grumpy old grouch is afraid of growing old.*

*S*ome of my most vivid memories are about my birthday
celebrations when I was a child. My adult cousins, Anna,
Ellen, and Alice, would mark each year by playfully tossing
me up in the air and catching me. It was three times when I
was three, four times when I was four, and five times when I
was five. "Don't ever grow old, Marilynn," they would say as
they threw me skyward. "Discover the secret. You be the one
who learns how to keep from growing old."

Solemnly I would promise, but inwardly I would wonder
what is so bad about growing old.

Even on Sunday

He's wrong, wrong, wrong! I thought. I was visiting a leading church in our community. The pastor, a fine, effective minister, was encouraging the members of the congregation to
reach out to the unchurched in the community. He exhorted
them to be willing to put up with the antics of children and
the problems of teens in order to win them. He explained that
if they were to reach unchurched adults, they would need to
be open and accepting. They must be willing to make changes

in their traditional worship so that it would be attractive for those they were attempting to reach. "We must make everyone welcome," he preached. "Everyone except for the old people. Old people aren't willing to change, and they can spoil everything we are trying to do." The options the pastor outlined later in the sermon showed he had done his homework well about church growth. Unfortunately, he had not kept up with the rapid changes that have been occurring in the age group over sixty.

I'm certain the pastor was not aware of his prejudice. It surprised me that this sincere minister, who really was concerned with reaching everyone in the community, was willing to write off a group with significant numbers. Allowances would be made for children, youth, and adults, but not for the old.

This pastor is not alone. How often have you heard friends speak approvingly of a church by saying, "There are so many young people there." Or they say, "It is wonderful to see a church with so many young families." How different it is if a church is filled with seniors! I know a congregation that has had a successful ministry reaching many people in their retirement years. The comment I hear most often about that church is "Too many old folks there!" Often people act as if there is something wrong with being old.

We all know times have changed. Our lives are different because of television, computers, the explosion of information, the increase in knowledge, and new inventions. What we eat, what we wear, and how we live is different from what it was fifty years ago. "Young people are not the same as they used to be," we often hear. True. But far greater changes have occurred in the age group over sixty, yet most people still think in terms of the stereotypes of fifty or even a hundred years ago. This is reflected in the connotations of the words we use to identify the last twenty or thirty years of our lives. Terms like *senior citizens, older Americans, retirees,* or *the golden years* suggest to many a time of failing health, restricted activities, and a rocking chair existence, a dreaded time of life.

Who Is Old?

In our changing times we can no longer judge age by the calendar. In the past, when people reached age sixty-five, they were designated as *old* for the purposes of retirement, Social Security, and tax considerations. However, newer laws are changing the figure to age seventy for Social Security. Does *old* change when congress passes new Social Security laws? Is a person old when she retires? Retirement age is no longer mandatory at age sixty-five. Many are working in their seventies and beyond, while the downsizing of companies has made it attractive for many people to retire after twenty or twenty-five years of service. A person cannot be considered old just because she is a "retiree." Some begin a second career. Others retire a second time and embark on a third career.

Can we judge by population trends? In 1790, only two percent of the population in America was age sixty-five or older. By 1994 that figure was thirteen percent, and it is still growing. Life expectancy has increased dramatically. At the beginning of our century it was forty-eight years. Now life expectancy has passed seventy-eight years and is still growing. What does that say about who is old?

Can we judge age by physical appearance? The other day I met a man who was bald, wrinkled, stooped, and bespectacled. He was only thirty-five years old. Often the physical attributes we associate with age are really the results of other factors, such as poor nutrition, lack of exercise, or the side effects of drugs. Persons in their eighties may be strong physically, vital mentally, and show no outward indications of aging.

Sherwood Wirt, the retired editor of *Decision* magazine, has said, "I don't know how old old is, but it's older than me!" Most people over sixty would agree. Today one may not grow "old" in becoming frail and being able to function until very shortly before death.

Everyone, whether two or one hundred two, is in the process of aging. From the moment we are born, we have started the miraculous experience of growing up. When we are younger, we look forward to birthdays and growing older. Why should it ever stop?

What's Wrong with Being Old?

In many cultures the old are honored. Isn't it curious the way so many Americans look at life? Americans think it is natural for a child to go through life's passages and become a teenager, then an adult. They think something is wrong if a child refuses to grow up. At the same time, they resist growing old. Carl Gustav Jung, the famous psychoanalyst, wrote, "To refuse to grow old is as foolish as to refuse to leave behind one's childhood." What makes us hesitant about growing older? Conventional wisdom still clings to the myth that we will grow old in much the same way as our parents did. That is not true. We need to correct the old myths about aging.

The Sick-Old-Lady Myth

Violet, a vigorous seventy-eight-year-old woman, was sent to the emergency room because she was very weak and dizzy. My husband, as the administrator of her retirement community, went to see how she was. "Her condition is poor," the emergency room doctor told him.

"What is your diagnosis?" my husband asked.

"She is old," the doctor replied.

"Old age is not a diagnosis. That is not her problem," my husband patiently pointed out.

"But she is seventy-eight years old," the doctor countered.

"A week ago this woman was the same age, but she was not weak and dizzy," Bill persisted. "She was active, vital, and energetic." Bill pushed the doctor to look further. He discovered that Violet was seeing more than one doctor and was over-medicated. When her medications were straightened out, Violet returned to her independent, busy life.

The emergency room doctor is not alone. Many people believe that age will catch up with a seventy-eight-year-old woman—in fact, people think it likely to happen much sooner.

This was the normal assumption in the past. After age sixty when symptoms or health problems came, people assumed it was a part of the irreversible decline called aging. Often their doctors agreed. They accepted sickness as a way of life for the rest of their days. That became a self-fulfilling prophecy.

Conventional wisdom still hangs on to the myth. In the past, fewer people lived past sixty-five, and many who did, suffered from poor health. That is no longer true. Because of many advances in medical science, today the average person can expect to live one-fourth of his or her life after the age sixty. Only ten percent of Americans sixty-five or older have a chronic health problem that restricts them from carrying on any major activity. This is the conclusion of current estimates from the National Health Interview Survey. The surprising truth is that most of us will live longer, healthier lives with many more satisfying options than were available to our parents.

How healthy we will be depends on our choices as well as our genes. The sooner we begin to take care of our bodies, the better-off we will be in our senior years. "If I had known I was going to live this long, I would have taken better care of myself," is a frequent comment of older people.

For those already in their senior years, common sense health rules apply. First, eat healthy, balanced meals. Malnutrition is a common cause of hospitalization for older Americans, especially those living alone. They usually intend to prepare good food for themselves, but the temptation is to do it the easy way, just for this meal. So they snack on crackers and cheese or peanut butter and put off preparing vegetables and other wholesome foods.

Exercise is the one most important factor to inhibit aging. Fortunately, it doesn't have to be strenuous exercise. Daily walks are ideal. The Cooper Institute for Aerobics Research in Dallas, Texas, has found that a person who walks regularly can cut her mortality rate in half. A woman who walks thirty minutes a day, six days a week will have a mortality rate almost as low as the athletic type who runs thirty or forty miles a week. It is never too late to begin exercising. Even people in their eighties and nineties who began to exercise were found to be more active, less depressed, and more involved in social activities. Working out not only strengthens muscles, but it helps brighten a person's outlook on life and gives one more energy for other tasks in life.

The Crabby Old Lady Myth

Yes, there are miserable old people who are set in their ways and who seem to try to make life wretched for those around them. There are also problem children, teens, and adults of all ages. It is unfair to stereotype people past retirement age as unhappy or difficult to get along with. The truth is that grumpy people tend to become grumpier as they age; nice people become nicer as they grow older. Not only that, but studies show that people with a positive attitude are healthier and live longer. The result is that a larger proportion of happy people are to be found among seniors than any other age group. Seniors have been getting a bad rap!

In many ways happiness is a habit. We develop patterns. Some see a glass as half empty while others see it as half full. In time, our outlook on life becomes established. The good news is that we can change. We can learn optimism. Our lives can become more joyful and satisfying if we follow the suggestions in this book. The sooner we begin, the easier it becomes.

The Crazy Old Lady Myth

Many people believe there is an inevitable decline in mental ability as the years pass. For most people this is one of their greatest fears. I certainly don't want to become a "dotty" old lady! Formerly it was thought that brain cells died in batches of hundreds of thousands perhaps even daily. Now neurobiologists have found that is not so. They have discovered that brain cells can shrink or grow dormant in old age. This is especially true if a person has given up mental stimulation or challenge. But even this can be reversed if people begin to use their brain power. Scientists call the process "sprouting." Even in later years new neural processes can form additional synapses.

Hugh Downs, of television fame, has good news. "The whole idea that older people don't learn as well is pure non-sense," he scoffs. "Maybe split-second brain functions slow down after about age forty-eight, but that is more than offset by acquired techniques, accumulated wisdom, and focus." This is not just one man's opinion. It is a part of what he learned at Mount Sinai Medical Center's outstanding gerontology pro-gram. He was accepted into their program at age seventy. When he completed the course, he was not able to be board certified because he was not a physician. Instead they decided to give him a Certificate in Geriatric Medicine. Today Hugh Downs is cochair of the Research and Education Committee in the Geriatric Advisory Council of the Mount Sinai Medical Cen-ter. His book, *Fifty to Forever,* a source book for living an active, involved, and fulfilling second half of life, has been a best-seller.

"My concentration has actually improved with age," Hugh Downs reports. Thousands of seniors enrolled in community courses would agree. Their increased motivation more than makes up for the slight decrease in rote memory ability.

You may not be as famous as Hugh Downs, but you can keep your mind sharp and continue to learn through the years. Reading is excellent exercise for the mind. Read the daily newspaper, read books, and read magazines (don't just flip through the pages). Do crossword puzzles. Balance your checkbook. Keep a journal. Write letters. Join a discussion group. Don't just passively watch television. Think!

The Stubborn-Old-Lady Myth

"What's wrong with old people?" I asked a group of young adults.

"They just won't change," came the answer. "They want everything to be the way it was in the good old days. They won't accept new ideas, and they live in the past."

Some older people are like that. There are those who keep everything in its place and never vary their routine. As these people grow older, these patterns tend to become more pronounced. Kathleen turned down an invitation to attend a bridal shower for her favorite granddaughter. The shower was to be held Friday afternoon, she explained, and that was the time she always had her hair done. Kathleen would not consider changing her hair appointment for any reason. Keeping to her regular routine reduced any risks she might have to take. One gerontologist calls this reasoning *life prevention*, and points out that people like Kathleen also lose something precious—the delightful possibility of pleasant surprises.

Are all older people like that? No, no, no! Some of the leaders of change in this world are seniors. Grandma Moses was over eighty when she took up art and dared to be different in her paintings. Think of Nelson Mandela, who in his seventies is leading his nation in its greatest time of change. Harlan Sanders was open to new ideas and began Colonel Sanders' Kentucky Fried Chicken franchises when he was past retirement age.

Let's be honest. There is a part of all of us that doesn't like change. It's one way we have of protecting ourselves against surprises. If we keep things the same, we don't have to worry about what might happen. Life becomes predictable and comfortable. We all do this in some areas of life, and within limits it's a healthy way to live. We tend to do things in the same order when we get up in the morning. We have a place we keep our toothbrush and we know where the toothpaste is. We prepare the morning coffeepot using the same amount of coffee. We don't stop after each activity to ask, "What will I do next?" Familiar patterns make life go more smoothly.

Some people never do establish routines. They cannot find their car keys because they never put them in the same place twice. They spend much time looking for things and deciding what to do next.

We don't have to choose either extreme. We are able to make the conscious choice to be open to change, enjoy new activities, and welcome new ideas while still keeping our moorings. We tend to notice the rigid old lady or the old woman who is unorganized. The majority of seniors have chosen a middle path, based on the wisdom they have accumulated through the years that leads to a healthy balance and a happy lifestyle.

The Lady-in-the-Rocking-Chair Myth

"Retirement ain't what it used to be," reporter Connie Goldman wrote after interviewing hundreds of seniors. "Who wants to sit in a rocking chair reminiscing about the good old days when so many other possibilities beckon?" The picture of the little old lady sitting in her rocking chair on the front porch is no longer typical, if it ever was. In fact, how long has it been since you have seen anyone sitting on her front porch?

There was a time when all that was open to grandmothers were household options: doing the dishes, doing the wash, ironing shirts and dresses, and spending several hours a day in the kitchen cooking and baking from scratch. It was after these things were done that an exhausted grandma might be found rocking. Of course, if she was too old to work, she might have nothing more to do than rock all day.

Women in the past were often old at age sixty-five. Today most women of sixty-five see themselves as being in their prime. They stuff the dirty plates and silver in the dishwasher and toss a load of clothes in the automatic washing machine. They probably have forgotten where the iron is, because they take care to buy only wash and wear. Convenience foods take little time to prepare, often in the microwave, or they may eat out in a fast-food restaurant.

What is there for women in their prime at sixty-five or older to do? Plenty, and they are not only finding it but many are having the time of their lives.

The Second Adulthood

The average forty-year-old American female reading this book can expect to live past her eighty-first birthday. A woman who reaches age fifty today—and remains free of cancer and heart disease—can expect to see her ninety-second birthday. If medical science continues to make the strides it has in the past, life expectancy can be expected to grow. This is a wonderful change from the past. It also has serious implications for those of us living today.

We cannot change that death is inevitable. We can change how we age. We can sit back and let aging happen to us, or we can make life happen for us. Experts say there is a clear distinction between passive aging and successful aging. Successful aging is much like a career choice. We choose the direction we want to go, decide on goals, and make commitments to ourselves about the strategies we intend to use.

Gail Sheehy, in her book, *New Passages*, writes that women today must plan for what she calls the second adulthood. She explains the average woman today will have as many adult years after age fifty as before. Most of these years will be lived in at least relatively good health. The tasks of the first adulthood include such markers as marriage, childbirth, first job, the empty nest, and hopefully some personal success at work or as a homemaker.

"What do I do with the rest of my life?" is the question women increasingly are asking as they enter their second adulthood. They ask questions like: *Do I really want to spend the next twenty years working at what I've been doing? Or do I really want to spend the next twenty or thirty years watching TV, planting bulbs, or playing bridge?*

This is a time when many women discover they do have real choices. When the "retirement" years come, a woman undergoes more dramatic changes in a shorter time than at any other period of life except childhood or adolescence. There are major shifts in her work and leisure time. More and more women are making positive choices. Today late bloomers are emerging everywhere. They are swelling the enrollments of community colleges. A large number of older women are earning professional degrees. The Elderhostels are filled with many thousands of seniors who often combine travel with learning about a myriad of subjects just because they are interesting. Many are competing in the Senior Olympics, while thousands of others have joined groups that exercise regularly. Some are tapping their keyboards, writing for fun or profit or writing their life review just for themselves. Many have begun their own business, doing something they love in the hope that money might follow. Everywhere you go, you find seniors working at part-time jobs. Often they are not working for the money. A woman who retires from a high-pressure position as an executive may be found working part-time for minimum wage at a nursery because she enjoys flowers and people.

The second adulthood is a time for volunteer activities. Many women who are still in the workplace enjoy volunteering. Those who are not employed find personal satisfaction and fulfillment in volunteer activities.

The Joy of Being Yourself

A most delightful opportunity presents itself during the second adulthood. We become increasingly free to be ourselves. At tea the other day, one of my older friends, with a twinkle in her eye, told me, "I'm not who I used to be, so I've got to figure out who I am now." She's right! It's impractical for us to try to respond to the afternoon of our life in the same way we did during its morning, the psychologist Carl Jung would point out.

"Active life demands a measure of conformity," wrote the perceptive Swiss physician Paul Tournier. "A man must play society's game if he is not to be rejected by society. He must act the conventional part that society imposes on him. But later on, the time comes to break from this social conditioning, when a man can rediscover his spontaneity and originality in order to become himself once more." This is equally true of women.

What freedom when we don't worry about advancement in the office or what the boss will think of how we dress. "When I grow old, I shall wear purple," is the opening essay of a popular book. Personally, I have no desire to wear purple. I do get excited about the concept the statement expresses—that in my mature years I can be myself. Even if what I choose may appear to others to be a little eccentric, one of the joys of aging is that in my older years, I will be allowed to get away with it. This applies to practically all of life: what I will eat, wear, read, choose to commit myself to, choose not to do, whom I will associate with, and what my passion in life will be. As we grow older, we become less and less alike. The older we grow, the more individual we become. How wonderful!

Henry David Thoreau observes, "We are constantly invited to be what we are." The second adulthood gives us the opportunity to discover who we are and to celebrate our uniqueness. That in itself is its own reward.

The Joy of Becoming Wiser

The second adulthood, and especially the later years, should be a time of increasing wisdom. Sheehy refers to the seventh decade of life "the sage seventies" and uses the term *sageing* instead of aging.

We learn from experience. In our older years, we have accumulated a lifetime of experience. Recent research shows that the mental skills of most people over seventy are still sharp, much sharper than most people think. This is a time when we begin to understand the broader meaning of life and to place things in focus. In our younger years, we need to learn facts to be competent in our occupation or tasks in life. Later in life, understanding becomes more important than data.

Regardless of our IQ, we can develop a wisdom that guides us in our outlook on life. We learn to accept life and the values of a generous mind and soul. Wisdom leads to forgiveness and the release of bitterness. Wisdom enables one to react to the conflicts, problems, and accidents of life in positive and constructive ways. This wisdom leads to a greater satisfaction in living. Often the older, wise woman can be a blessing to others in her life. She has the ability to share insights, place events in perspective, and keep her focus on the main thing, which often is love and relationships.

Oriental cultures for centuries have celebrated their elders because they recognized the wisdom that the years bring. Let growing wiser be one of your joys as you grow older. "Sageing" has its own reward.

The Joy of Maturity

When my friends learned I was writing this book, many of them shared helpful material with me. How good it is to have friends! I found I had a whole stack of inspirational writings on how to remain youthful. Interestingly, they thought the message of *How to Become a Sweet Old Lady* was going to be "How to stay youthful and not become an old lady." Usually the message of the inspirational writings they sent me was "think young."

Now I agree with the idea these cute, inspirational pieces are encouraging, but a fatal flaw to such reasoning needs to be pointed out. A sixty-year-old-person ought not try to think like a teenager. Why should we encourage an octogenarian to think like a twenty-year-old girl? The myth is that youthful thinking is good and seasoned, adult thinking is bad. The myth is that youthful thinking is fun, creative, exciting. It sees possibilities. Adult thinking is stodgy, predictable, and boring.

We need to contradict firmly such ideas. As we grow older, we have the opportunity to be even more creative in our thinking. Years of experience give one the background to see additional options. The wild-eyed impracticability of youth is replaced by the seasoned judgment of maturity that can save a person from many false starts and failures. The mature thinker has the advantage of being able to dream as when she was younger. Now she has the resources and the ability to network that can make more dreams come true. And speaking of fun—most older adults would not want to change places with today's young people. They are enjoying life more than they did in their younger years because they are thinking like mature adults. Are a lot of older adults really enjoying life more? I found this to be universally true with the many people

I talked to, and my findings are confirmed by a number of scientific studies.

Occasionally we see an older woman who dresses like a teen, styles her hair like a teen, and tries to talk like a teen. *How sad,* we think. No one commends her for thinking, acting, and looking youthful. "She should act her age," people say. Of course.

It's great to act young in our youth. But the zest for life, creativity, fun, and new, wonderful ideas do not end as we grow older. They grow better if we mature wisely. That's what this book is about. Maturity is a wonderful trait that can only be fully developed as we age.

TWENTY

❦

Wear Out,
Don't Rust Out

*A sweet old lady stays active all her life. A
grumpy old grouch sits and rocks.*

C an you be ready in fifteen minutes?" It was my friend
Bardy on the telephone. "I need your help. I'll be by to
pick you up in my car."

"Where are we going?" I asked. "What should I wear?"

"It really doesn't matter. You'll see. Or I should say, I'll see."
Her infectious laughter crackled across the telephone lines,
then the dial tone alerted me that she assumed my willingness
to accompany her on some secret mission. If my hunch was
correct, she was probably already out the door, in her car, and
headed in my direction.

For what? I had learned not to try to second-guess my
friend. Bardy is the most interesting person I know—and the
most unpredictable. She had always wanted to be a registered
nurse, so she went back to school and became one when she
was sixty-three years old. "The real fun started when I graduated," Bardy had informed me. "When I applied for jobs, I was
told, 'We retire people at your age, Mrs. Bardarson, we don't
hire them!'"

Disappointed but not discouraged, Bardy told God that if
he didn't want her sidelined, he'd have to help her find her

niche. She continued to apply for nursing positions and finally was hired by a retirement home. She was an instant hit with the residents. When they talked with her about their aches and pains, they found a sympathetic ear. After all, she had many of those aches and pains herself. They could tell she loved her work and that she was genuinely concerned for them. When she did retire at age seventy, the residents gave her the biggest party in the history of the retirement home.

Soon Bardy was at my front door. "I'm driving today," she announced. "Jump in the passenger's seat."

"Where are we going?" I queried as I locked the front door of our house.

"It doesn't matter," she replied with a Cheshire grin on her face. "Marilynn, you know I had to retire from nursing when it became too much for me to lift the patients. Now I've found a new job. I'm going to travel with blind tourists. I'll get to go to all the places I've wanted to see. I'll be helping others, and I'll even get paid for it! Now I need you to help me prepare. Close your eyes while I drive."

I complied.

"Are your eyes closed? Good!" Bardy said. "I have to practice." She began to describe the scenery of the Seattle streets as she would to a blind tourist. From time to time she would interrupt herself to ask me, "Could you picture that? Was I clear? Did I make sense? Do I sound condescending?"

That day I saw Seattle in a new way. I learned one of Bardy's secrets as well. What makes her such an interesting person is her determination to wear out, not rust out.

The Golden Mean

Here I must hasten to observe that the mature person is one who has learned to find a healthy balance in life. An earlier chapter discussed the importance of taking time to smell the roses. It dealt with the serious condition many have of being too busy. This chapter acknowledges that many have the opposite need. They do too little. Either one of these choices is a problem. Maturity is discovering what the ancient Greeks called "the golden mean"—the middle ground.

The metaphor of rusting out is an apt description. If we do not use our minds, they become slow and sluggish. If we become couch potatoes, our bodies soon lose their muscular tone and other organs begin to atrophy. If we do not use our talents, we will lose them. A musician grows rusty without practice. A good cook will lose many of her skills if she stays out of the kitchen. "Use it or lose it," is a popular adage, and the conventional wisdom it is based upon is true.

When we say *wear out,* we don't mean *break down.* There is a difference. I love the little hand mixer I use in my kitchen. It's one of the most useful tools I have, and I have been using it for years. I do not use it when I bake bread, however. It was never meant to mix heavy bread dough, and if I attempted to use it in this way, it would soon overheat and break down. Used properly, my little mixer will last for years. Not forever, of course. Normal wear, in time, will take its toll. One day I will have to discard this trusty kitchen helper, but when the time comes, I will do it with affection. Together we will have prepared so many good things, and I will recognize that it has worn well.

God has designed us so that we can have a full and mean-ingful life. Overwork will result in burnout, exhaustion, and collapse. Too little activity will lead to decay. A proper balance produces satisfaction and fulfillment. This is the message we mean to convey when we say *wear out, don't rust out.*

Bardy's story is an illustration of this principle. When she reached sixty, she did not stop living. She fulfilled her dream of becoming a nurse, and she persisted until she found a rewarding place of service. She was realistic. She did not try to push herself beyond her capabilities. When at seventy she found the physical requirements of nursing to be too demand-ing, she did not try to continue. Rather, she found another rewarding occupation within the limits of her health and strength—traveling with the blind.

This lesson is one we all need to take to heart, regardless of our age. Life is constantly changing. Our success and happiness are determined to a large measure by the way we handle life's transitions. As we move from childhood to the teen years, then to young adulthood and midlife, by the very nature of things some activities stop. How sad when a girl who has been active in many activities in her school years retreats to doing little more than working a nine-to-five routine job. Too many capable women, when they become mothers, talk only of diapers and baby bottles. Don't misunderstand. Nothing is more challenging than being a mother. No occupation is more important than motherhood. A baby needs more than a bottle filler and a diaper changer. A good mother is a person who continues to grow as a person. This is not only vital for her mental and emotional health, but it is also necessary if she is to do her best as a parent.

Grow into maturity. Make wise choices. Wear out, don't rust out.

TWENTY ONE

You Can Do It

Sarah had a gift for finding flaws. Usually her criticisms were accurate and her objections were right on the mark. Still, her constant negative comments kept her from getting close to others. As I gave my talk, "How to Become a Sweet Old Lady Instead of a Grumpy Old Grouch," I worried about Sarah's response. I was not surprised that she was one of the first to make her way up to me at the close of the meeting.

"You had several good points in your speech," she began. "But . . ."

There was a long pause. I waited for the inevitable critique.

"But . . ." she began again, then paused. I was aware she was having difficulty trying to express what she was about to say. Finally she blurted out, "But you can't teach an old dog new tricks. I would like to be different, but I'm just too old to change."

I had never seen Sarah so sincere, so genuine. She really did want to be a sweet old lady.

"Sarah, do you want to change?" I asked gently.

"More than you would ever think," she replied. "But it's too late. The old habits are too strong to break."

I sent up an SOS prayer that the Lord would give me the words I needed. "I understand what you're saying," I replied. "It's so hard to change, but we can. Everyone can change."

"Maybe you can, but I can't," Sarah insisted. "I know. I'm stuck with myself. I've given up even trying."

"You may be a puzzle to yourself, Sarah, but do you think that God, who created the world and made you, is baffled by your problems and is unwilling to help you? Of course not!"

Suddenly it became clear to her, and Sarah responded with a powerful insight. "I guess our real sin is to be stuck with ourselves and refuse to change. That's not going to happen to me."

People were surprised as a different Sarah gradually emerged. A new friendliness began to replace her old, somewhat prickly personality. Encouragement supplanted criticism. Helpfulness took the place of criticism. Women recognized the wisdom that Sarah always had, but now her ideas were accepted because they were phrased without their former hostile wrappings.

A few years have passed. Sarah is now the president of the active women's group of her church. People enjoy being with her, and she has found a new enjoyment of life.

It's Your Choice

None of us needs to be stuck with ourself when God has a better idea. He will help us make our choices. Choices repeated become habits. Habits become crystalized into character. Often, individual decisions seem insignificant, but added together they determine our lifestyle.

This book is an invitation to a fascinating pilgrimage. It is a guide to a lifelong process whose goal is Christian maturity. That's what becoming a sweet old lady is really about. In the pages of this book you have met a number of fellow travelers. For the most part, they have been ordinary women facing the most commonplace problems and typical life stiuations. Their stories have helped us see that life is a many-splendored thing. The jewel of maturity is multifaceted. A sweet old lady (or the woman of any age we enjoy being with) is a person with many desirable characteristics, not just one outstanding trait.

I trust you were affirmed as you read passages in this book and recognized that you possess the strengths that were described. It is often more difficult to identify our shortcomings, but everyone, especially this author, has weaknesses, areas in our lives that need help. Some changes can be made if we decide to change. You can decide to make new friends, accentuate the positive, try new things, create your own party, and develop a vital faith.

There are other changes for which you may need God's help. For example, if you are bitter or resentful and there is someone you can't forgive, then you will need God's help with this disagreeable person. God can help you and wants to help you. God's will is never for anyone to become a grumpy old grouch. It is always to become more Christlike, to become more and more a sweet old lady.

After I talked to a mother-daughter banquet, one little girl came up to me and said, "When I get old, I want to be just like my grandmother."

That's one of the joys of becoming a sweet old lady.

The Sweet
Old Lady's Secrets

A sweet old lady is constantly changing for the better. A grumpy old grouch tries to change other people.

A sweet old lady takes the initiative. A grumpy old grouch complains that nothing interesting is happening.

A sweet old lady admires the roses. A grumpy old grouch complains about the thorns.

A sweet old lady is an active participant in life. A grumpy old grouch lets life pass her by.

A sweet old lady does what she can with what she has. A grumpy old grouch quits if everything does not work out.

A sweet old lady works around her limitations. A grumpy old grouch says, "I can't!"

A sweet old lady has learned to wait expectantly. A grumpy old grouch is impatient.

A sweet old lady keeps doing what is needed. A grumpy old grouch gives up easily.

A sweet old lady knows when to quit. A grumpy old grouch must be forced out.

A sweet old lady takes time to enjoy life. A grumpy old grouch is too busy complaining.

A sweet old lady makes new friends. A grumpy old grouch complains all her friends are gone.

A sweet old lady encourages. A grumpy old grouch criticizes.

A sweet old lady is kind. A grumpy old grouch is selfish.

A sweet old lady forgives. A grumpy old grouch holds grudges.

A sweet old lady gives beautiful memories. We try to forget a grumpy old grouch.

A sweet old lady has a healthy sense of humor. A grumpy old grouch finds her life to be grim.

A sweet old lady develops a vital faith. A grumpy old grouch ignores God.

A sweet old lady is content. A grumpy old grouch has many complaints.

All of life is cherished by a sweet old lady. A grumpy old grouch is afraid of growing old.

A sweet old lady is active all her life. A grumpy old grouch sits and rocks.

To contact Marilynn Carlson Webber for
speaking engagements, write or call

Marilynn Carlson Webber
275 Celeste Drive
Riverside, CA 92507
(909) 784-4313